Fatherless Fathering

A Practical Guide for Men and Women Who Lacked the
Benefit of Being Properly Raised by a Father

Jay Cameron

Renown Publishing

Fatherless Fathering / Jay Cameron
ISBN-13: 978-1-945793-98-1

This book is dedicated: to everyone who made a deposit into my life and helped to shape me into the man that I am becoming—I thank you.

To my mother, Cindy Speller—
Who sacrificed her dreams so that I could live mine.

To my wife, Latricia—
For being the best mother my children could have ever hoped for. Thank you for also being an incredible wife and for supporting me when I win and when I lose. There is no price tag I can place on your level of commitment on this journey.

To my grandmother, Verdell Glover—
Who personified unconditional love.

To Mrs. Vera White and Mrs. Deborah Holmes—
For seeing in me what no one else did
(and for forcing me to do it!).

Finally, to my four children, who have served as the inspiration for this book, Taylor, Eric, Jayson, and Justin—
The four of you hold a special place in my heart and in my life. You are the reason I'm the father I am today. I hope that you will always be proud to say, "That's my daddy."
I also pray that your children and the generations to come will know that this book was written as a gift to them.

CONTENTS

The Real, Uncut Story 3

Give Your Child an Identity 59

Transition from Untrained to Trained................... 67

Breaking the Family Cycle 79

The Importance of Wisdom 95

Make the Most of Your Time 101

Exercising Common Sense 107

A New Day 119

Questions 129

Additional Resources 130

About the Author 131

The Real, Uncut Story

Before we start, I want to encourage you to get ready for an honest account that chronicles my journey toward healthy fatherhood. It's real. It's raw. I also believe it's a story many will relate to. At first I was hesitant about sharing so much about my life, but there are countless people who need to read it exactly the way it happened. They need it uncut and unfiltered, and that is exactly what they will receive.

Understanding the context of my story will give you a greater understanding of the transformation that has occurred, and I hope that it will give you inspiration with your own parenting journey. Parenting is hard, but it is something you will do for a lifetime. I learn something new every day. I have made lots of mistakes, but these mistakes did not deter me from being the best father I could be. This book is for men and women who lacked proper training from a father. My hope is that my journey will encourage you to be the best parent you can be.

How We Were Raised

You may have been fortunate enough to have grown up with present parents in your life. They attended your ball games. They saw to it that you made it to school with your homework completed. They packed your lunch, encouraged you to go to college, and equipped you with the things you needed to transition into adulthood, as best as they could.

They weren't perfect. They made some mistakes, and there are some things you wish they would have done differently. Overall, though, they did a great job of raising you to be capable and confident, and you now have the tools you need to parent your own kids and guide them toward success.

Some of you may have grown up in a household where both parents were physically present, but emotionally absent. Some of you had parents who were ill-equipped to teach you the proper life lessons. They simply didn't know because no one taught them, or maybe they chose to ignore the good lessons they were taught. Perhaps the lessons they did teach or model for you were not positive lessons. You may have had parents who suffered from substance abuse or who were physically abusive to you or another member of your family. Perhaps your parents were preoccupied with their own lives (i.e., relationships, careers, education, etc.) and you were left to fend for yourself.

Or you may be like me. You may have grown up with an absent father, an overworked mother, and a community of people who modeled bad behavior and poor decision making. Now you're a parent, and you're struggling. You feel untrained for the task at hand, and you see your relationship with your child slipping away.

Here's the good news: It doesn't matter if you came from a beautiful home with healthy, parent role models or a one-room apartment with an absent father (or mother) whose name you didn't even know. *You can be a great parent.* Your father may have been absent, but you don't have to be. Your mother may have been abusive, but you don't have to be. You can improve your relationship with your child and break the cycle of bad parenting.

Motherless Mothering

The title of this book could easily have been *Motherless Mothering.* Many men and women who lacked the benefit of being properly raised by a mother will be able to relate to the challenges I faced as a fatherless child. Unfortunately, many people did not have the benefit of being properly raised by both parents (or either parent, in some cases). Perhaps you had a great father but your mother was absent in one form or another. Perhaps you are still dealing with the effects of a toxic mother who physically raised you but emotionally neglected or abused you.

Most daughters long for a mother's love, guidance, nurturing, and acceptance. Most sons long for their mother's comfort, support, and encouragement. Many people automatically assume that because mothers are usually the primary caregivers, their parenting style is healthy. Some of the most mother-deficient environments are headed up by present-but-absent mothers. Those relationships can carry strife well into the adult years. Many adult children have had to establish healthy boundaries to deal with the toxicity of one or both parents. Whatever your childhood situation might have been, there is hope moving forward.

The Journey Begins

I was born in Charleston, South Carolina, in 1972. Life was great early on, or at least that's how I felt. I was supported by my mother, grandmother, grandfather, and aunt. But around the age of four or five, I realized there was a huge void in my life: my father was absent. And though my grandfather was around, he was quiet, passive, and disconnected. I learned later that his father wasn't around for him when he was young, either.

Much of what I learned as a boy came from the women in my life. They taught me how to process thoughts and emotions and how to deal with challenges. They were a loud, vocal, emotional bunch, and this impacted me. It taught me to make a scene and to be aggressive to get my way.

D.C.-Bound

When I was four years old, my mother moved to Washington, D.C. She landed a job with a congressman from South Carolina. She saw the opportunity to move me into a new environment with more opportunities than what Charleston (or more specifically, a little suburb called Summerville) offered at the time.

Meeting J.D. for the First Time

When I was seven years old, I met my father, J.D. (aka Joseph Daniel) for the first time. As I held my mother's hand at the Federal Center Southwest Metro Station in Washington, D.C., I saw a stranger approaching us. I gripped her hand tighter. She leaned down and said, "This is your dad." I remember thinking he was old because he had gray hair. I don't recall much else from that first encounter, aside from my mom asking me to give him a kiss on the cheek as we said goodbye. I still remember how awkward I felt and the stubble on his cheek.

I didn't see him again until I was ten years old, but the longing I had begun to feel for my dad when I was four or five grew over the years. I was very aware that I had a father somewhere out there, but he just wasn't in my life. I remember crying at nine years old, wondering why my father wouldn't come to see me. What had I done wrong? What was wrong with me? These were the feelings I was trying to process as a nine-year-old.

I heard so much about my dad over the years—that people loved him, that he did cool stuff, that he was a great negotiator. Even though I didn't really know him, I was so proud to be his son.

At some point, we finally made arrangements for him to come visit me, but he didn't show. I waited and waited. He had promised to pick me up. Nothing. No call. No notice. Just—nothing. I was extremely disappointed and realized that I was not important in his life. You can imagine what this did to my self-image and self-worth. As a child, I could only conclude that if my own father didn't want a relationship with me, I must have done something wrong. I must have been *less than*.

Eventually, we did begin meeting on an occasional basis. When we met, the meetings were awkward and inauthentic. Our meetings were always in public at fast-food restaurants. It did not make sense to me why I could not simply go spend the night at my father's house. Why did we have to meet at McDonald's? Why did I only have his office phone number? I felt like I was a secret. To a ten-year-old child, it did not make sense. Actually, it still does not make sense after all of these years.

As a result of my father's inconsistencies and broken promises, seeds of anger, bitterness, and insecurities were planted in me. Eventually, I lost hope that I'd ever have a father. I felt rejected and abandoned. Those feelings stayed for a long, long time.

I became destructive. I blamed my mother for my father's absence, and I had explosive arguments with her. I flipped tables and threw things. I used the worst kinds of profanity toward her. My outbursts got so bad that she had to call the police on occasion. I didn't understand why I was so filled with rage. I had behavioral issues at school, too, and I was at the bottom of my grade-school classes. The school tried to help and attempted to diagnose me, but I remained uncontrollable. I formed a wall around myself as protection from the outside world. Nobody's opinions, advice, or critiques mattered. I was all about self-preservation. Anger had made me numb to the feelings and well-being of others.

Due to lack of financial support from my father, my mother was forced to take a job that required her to be away from home in the evenings. This was her only option, but she recognized it wasn't a good situation for me. In an effort to help me, it was agreed that I would move back to South Carolina with my grandparents.

I was eleven years old and ready for something new. Everything was exciting at first. I had always wanted to move back to South Carolina, but little did I know that this would prove to do more harm than good.

Because of my emotional deficiencies, I was vulnerable and seeking some form of acceptance and validation. I found myself in a series of bad relationships, from the age of eleven until twenty-one. These relationships were sexual in nature. I had no one to help me navigate the hormones of puberty and the emotions of my adolescent years. With the collapse of each relationship, my feelings of inadequacy would compound.

At the age of eleven, I became sexually active with a girl who was two years older. We lived next door to each other, so it was easy for her to sneak out of the window at night so that we could have sex. She was controlling and dealing with her own issues. I will never forget the day she thought I spoke to another girl on the school bus and, in a fit of rage, she slapped me five or six times in front of all of the other students. Embarrassment, anger, fear, and shame set in. I felt tremendous rage as she was slapping me, but I also felt helpless and trapped in the moment. Everything in me wanted to defend myself, but I could not bring myself to hit a girl. I sat there and took the humiliation of being slapped multiple times by a girl for something I had not done. The other students laughed at me, and the bus driver did not stop the assault.

I remember the familiar feeling that something was wrong with me being reinforced as I got off the bus that day. Because I did not have my father or any other man to help me navigate such territory, I was left to my own thoughts and immature reasoning. This day was pivotal because it added another layer to the feelings I already had about myself. Because of my feelings of inadequacy and lack of relationship experience, I stayed in this abusive relationship for several more years. Her actions that day opened the door to verbal and physical abuse.

When I was twelve years old, my anger boiled over and I decided that I was going to stop the humiliation by setting her on fire the next time she was physically abusive. My friends knew of my plan and were waiting for the big showdown. As I was preparing, I poured the gasoline into a foam cup. I didn't know that gasoline melts foam, which thankfully ruined my plan. Almost simultaneously, a police officer shined his light in my face, so my plan was completely thwarted. Someone had tipped off the police to my scheme, but since no crime had been committed and the evidence melted away, there were no charges filed. It was at this point that I began to sense that my feelings and actions came from something a lot deeper. I still did not have anyone to talk to, though, and my problems continued.

I was afraid to speak up for myself because I was afraid of confrontation. I would suppress my feelings until they reached a boiling point, and then I would explode. This mode of responding to disagreement and conflict would persist for many years.

To make matters worse, the majority of the male examples in my life battled some form of addiction, whether it was alcohol, women, or drugs. There were a few men who set a positive example for me, and I will remember them fondly, but it was the negative examples who were closest to me. They simply drowned out what few positive influences existed in my life.

I took out my anger on anything I felt I could control. I also focused my anger toward animals, catching and torturing them to death. I knew this was wrong, but I felt an incredible sense of satisfaction each time I did it. It was almost like a sick high. I didn't understand why I got satisfaction out of doing this, and there was no one to talk to because of the embarrassment and shame I felt.

I was also a bully, who would verbally abuse and fight smaller kids who couldn't and wouldn't fight back. No one was aware of my bullying, since I targeted people I knew would keep quiet. I was terribly unhappy, but I couldn't understand why I was unhappy.

Please understand, the failures of my father and the absence of my mother are not excuses for toxic behaviors. I remember justifying acting out because of my issues with my father and mother, but this was wrong. The only person I could really blame was myself.

While I was living with my grandparents, my grades and behavior continued to spiral downward. In eighth grade, I was suspended from school four times and told that another suspension would result in an expulsion. This was a wake-up call for me because it was the first time I was being held accountable for my actions. I was used to getting my way no matter how poor my behavior was. As a result, it was agreed that at the end of that school year, I would return to Washington, D.C., to live with my mother.

I share all of this because it is important to understand where certain behaviors I developed over the years began. Who would have thought that a twelve-year-old could be involved in so much? My life had spiraled out of control, and no one knew what to do. In fact, because I had learned how to hide things, no one truly knew the depth of my issues.

My father's absence was not the only factor contributing to my rage. I harbored anger and resentment toward my mother and blamed her, on many levels, for his absence. My anger toward my mother was also rooted in her refusal to allow me to cut my hair. It sounds silly, perhaps, but there it is. As I said in the beginning, you are getting the whole story, not a shiny version.

In the early 1980s, the Jeri Curl was a popular hairstyle. My mother forced me to put a chemical relaxer in my hair to create the style. I hated the process because the relaxer burned my scalp and left scabs, which then turned into large flakes. I couldn't help but think that there was something unnatural about this process. It left me wondering why women would willingly put themselves through this on a monthly basis.

The most humiliating part was how it made me appear: I looked like a girl. I was teased by my peers and approached by guys who thought I was a girl. It was one of the lowest points of my life because I was a boy who wanted to look like a boy. I was a boy who did not like being approached by guys. My mother was abandoning me to a fate of bullying and confusion. Deep resentment set in toward my mother, but it also contributed to my resentment of my father.

I felt that my dad would have protected me from my

mother's refusal to allow me to get my hair cut. Once again, he was absent, and it was another stab into my heart, which was quickly hardening from the rejection. To my adolescent mind, I was being abandoned by both of my parents, and there was nothing I could do to stop it.

Spoiled Rotten

My family did not hold me accountable for my behavior, so I pushed the limits. At age thirteen, I was stealing the family car at night and going for joy rides. One day, after getting suspended from the school bus, I decided to drive my go-kart to school in protest. It was illegal to drive a go-kart on public roads, but at every turn, I was never held accountable, which communicated to me that I was in control.

I also learned how to manipulate my mother and grandmother. I would do just enough to appear as if I were changing and then do something outrageous. I believe they felt sorry for me and attempted to appease my feelings by letting things slide. They also gave me whatever I wanted. Maybe they hoped having more things would make up for not having a father.

Coming to Blows

My relationship with my aunt and grandfather reached an all-time low after my aunt attacked me due to my rebellious attitude and I responded by throwing her into a mirror. My aunt and I frequently came to blows, but she had always won because I was just a kid. She never put her hands on me again, though, after I threw her into the mirror.

My grandfather, who had been physically present but emotionally absent most of my life, responded by threatening to shoot me, so I cursed him out. Our relationship was never the same after that day, and I lost all respect for him. It was clear that it was time for me to move back to live with my mother.

After moving back to Washington, D.C., though, things did not get better. My father called more, but my heart had hardened toward him. I lost interest in establishing a relationship with him. His negative track record had guaranteed that.

I started ninth grade at Jefferson Junior High School with the same attitude I ended eighth grade with. Little did I know that I was about to have an encounter that would change my life forever.

One day at school, the principal, Vera White, caught me in the hallway after the class bell rang. She warned me about my tardiness, but it was my comment in response to her that landed me in her office. Still, I wasn't concerned, because I was used to being in trouble. That is, I wasn't concerned until she informed me that I was suspended and if I wanted to return, I had to call my father and inform him of my actions. It was as if she knew the root of many of my issues and had called it out.

My heart sank—and I was terrified! I was afraid that if my behavior issues were exposed to my father, he would reject me completely. I tried to come up with every excuse, but Mrs. White would not budge. She marched me to the guidance counselor, Mrs. Hill, who made the call. It was a moment I will never forget.

When I spoke to my father on the phone in Mrs. Hill's office, he was not mean or even angry. Quite the opposite. He was gentle, but firm, and it was the first time he expressed his expectations of me in a way that seemed genuine. It's not an exaggeration to say that it was inspirational. And it worked. Mrs. White's decision to involve my father ended my school behavioral issues at Jefferson. My grades drastically improved, and things appeared to be on the upswing—at least for a bit.

My time at Jefferson was pivotal because I discovered something I did well: public speaking. As Mrs. White was correcting my actions, she and Mrs. Deborah Holmes discovered that I had the ability to speak well in public. I'd had no clue. No one had ever told me I had this ability until those two women noticed it. As a result, they gave me (non-voluntary) speaking opportunities in school.

My first big speaking engagement was running for student government treasurer for D.C. public schools. Not my school, mind you, but the regional position! I was beyond terrified because I had never spoken in front of an audience before, yet there was something inside of me that knew I needed to embrace this challenge. The process involved writing, memorizing, rehearsing, and delivering my speech in front of a group of my peers. With fear, trembling, and a very dry mouth, I did it.

To this day, I can still feel the emotions of delivering my first speech. Although I lost the election by one vote, I started to gain something much more valuable: confidence. After that event, I spoke in competitions at the South Korean Embassy, Concerned Black Men (an organization my father claimed he was a part of), and commencement ceremonies. My life as a public speaker had begun. Mrs. White and Mrs. Holmes had unlocked the rest of my life, and I will forever be grateful to them for forcing me to speak in public.

Despite all of the positive changes happening in my life, and the positive public image I was creating, I kept a dark side hidden. It seemed very easy to do, as long as I didn't get caught. A few days before my ninth-grade graduation, I was arrested at gunpoint for shoplifting. Because I was fourteen years old and considered a minor, the charges were dropped, but my family and personality problems had not been resolved. My father was still breaking promises, my mother was extremely emotional and out of answers, and I was still angry and out of control. In addition, I had a major issue with accepting responsibility for my actions. Blame was my game, which would prove to be my downfall later in life. As it turned out, I would discover that I was much like my father.

I had two circles of friends. Most of us faced similar absent-father challenges. We even called ourselves "the Capitol Park Bastards." We would laugh about it, but inside we were all longing for our fathers. One group was clean-cut, focused on education and on accomplishing something positive, while the other group was the complete opposite.

With my negative circle of friends, I found myself going deeper into the criminal life. From breaking into neighbors' homes while they were at work to randomly attacking people as they were walking down the street, we were headed down a path that was considered normal for many young black men in the 1980s. The crazy part is that I did not grow up in the "hood," but I had the "hood" mentality in me and was the ringleader of much of the madness. I will never forget the time one of my friends held me back from going off on a police officer. I was hurling profane words at the officer when my friend Sergio came to calm me down. The rage had gotten to the point that I no longer respected real authority.

Despite the brief upward swing during junior high school, my high school years saw my grades tank to the point of barely graduating. Some onlookers probably found this strange. After all, I had mastered public charisma and speaking. I won homecoming king and numerous superlatives my senior year. But in spite of those achievements, I walked across the stage with a 1.68 grade point average and no direction for my life. While I projected public confidence, internally I was still ruled by insecurities, anger, and fears.

By this time, my anger toward my father had also reached its peak. It shames me now, but I plotted to have him attacked as he walked from the metro station to the bus stop. My negative friends were the perfect bunch to accomplish this goal. We strategized and planned, and it consumed me day and night.

Shortly before the attack was to occur, I mentioned it to my mother. I expected her to possibly cosign without cosigning, but she surprised me. "He's not worth it," she said simply. When she said it, I heard her wisdom speaking. He wasn't worth it, and it would most likely impact my life forever. I canceled the plan—one of the few wise decisions I made at that age.

It would be easy to leave out this part of my story. I know, however, that sharing the hard-core places I came from will offer deeper insight into my transformation.

Teen Life

I found myself in the most trouble during the summer. Sneaking over to girls' houses to have sex while their parents were at work or inviting them to my home while my mother was at work was a normal activity. This was so common that I lost count of how many houses I snuck into while parents were at work. The final straw was when I found myself jumping out of a second-story window when a mother came home unexpectedly. Instead of going to her room to sleep, she decided to sleep on the sofa right next to the front door. The only path of escape was out of the second-story window. This was the day I vowed never to find myself in such a position again.

High School Toxic Love

My high school years also opened the door to one of the most toxic relationships of my life. Oftentimes, toxic people will attract other toxic people, and that is exactly what happened with us. She was adopted, and her adoptive parents divorced when she was very young. Her adoptive mother became an alcoholic, while her adoptive father remarried and started a new life and family. We both were dealing with severe rejection issues but did not know how to manage the feelings, which was a recipe for disaster.

The relationship began with all of the positive emotions and physical energy typical of two hormone-filled teenagers. Things progressed emotionally and sexually very quickly. We both experienced a level of comfort and acceptance we had never felt before. As quickly as the relationship advanced, though, it declined at the same rapid pace. We found ourselves addicted to each other, and no amount of reason could break through the toxic situation in which we found ourselves. By the time the relationship ended six years later, the drama had spanned from D.C. to Atlanta to Augusta and back to D.C., with incidents and situations including nearly coming to blows with her father, being threatened by her brothers, dropping out of college, a pregnancy that mysteriously ended, thousands of wasted dollars, and at least for me, contemplating suicide. It was bad.

As I will share in detail, breaking free from this relationship was incredibly difficult. I had invested so much of my life into it that I was determined it would be successful at any cost. I couldn't see that this relationship was hopeless and beyond repair. Or, maybe, I simply refused to see. It was one of the lowest periods of my life. It was also a pivotal moment because for the first time, I had to own my decisions.

The Confrontation

After my high school graduation at age seventeen, I'd had enough with my father keeping me a secret. I went to my father's house and knocked on the door. A young man, about fourteen years old, answered. My dad wasn't home, so I said, "Tell him his son Jay stopped by."

The boy looked shocked. "Who?"

"Jay. His son. Tell him I stopped by."

The boy opened the door wider. "You must be mistaken. He doesn't have a son named Jay."

I pulled out my ID to show him. He was in disbelief. His sister—my sister—peeked her head into the doorway and said, "I believe you. You look like him."

These were my half-siblings. They didn't even know I existed. Our father didn't have the decency or courage to tell them about me and about the other children he'd fathered and abandoned. Now I understood why I was a secret. The hardest part for me was when my father would tell me that he knew what he did was wrong and would promise to do better. For years he promised to welcome me into his home and into his new family, but he never did. So I showed up unannounced at his apartment.

After I met my siblings, I sat in the parking lot, waiting for my dad to get home. After he parked and got out of the car, I called out to him. I addressed him as "Mr." and not as "Dad," because we didn't have a father/son relationship. He didn't even recognize me. I reminded him who I was. He acted as if he was glad to see me and began his usual stuttering small talk that was laced with "ah" and "uh" as he tried to gather his thoughts. As we were talking in the parking lot, one of his neighbors walked up, and they briefly spoke. When he didn't introduce me, it was yet another stab in the heart.

When I informed my father that I'd met my three younger siblings, he maintained his composure, but I could see the brief look of shock on his face. I made it clear that I wanted to have a relationship with him and my siblings. He verbally agreed that it was long overdue and asked me to call him to set up another time to meet with the entire family.

He never answered my calls.

I tried to connect with my brother, but my father blocked every attempt. He forbade my brother from seeing me. A part of me understands it now: he had so many lies to cover up, and I was aware of many of them. For my part, I was angry and in no place to be a big brother to a fourteen-year-old boy. I would have been a bad role model to a boy who was quietly dealing with his own issues with our father. But my dad's absenteeism—his refusal to reach out to me and his rejection—reinforced those thoughts and feelings that something was wrong with me and that *I* was broken.

Shortly after I introduced myself to my younger siblings, I moved to Atlanta to attend college. The responsibility of living on my own proved to be too much, and I was evicted from my apartment. Poor financial and roommate choices do that. I irresponsibly spent all of my mother's money, ruined my credit, and found myself in a hole that would take years to climb out of.

Out of desperation, I lined up a job as a trash man. When my mother heard, she vehemently expressed her displeasure. She asked me to call my dad. She said he knew people in Atlanta who could help me secure better employment. So I did.

He promised to get back to me that same day, but he never did.

Time to Move On

I was done. That was the day I ended my pursuit of an active relationship with my dad. That was the day I decided to divorce my father once and for all. I couldn't do it anymore. I couldn't strive to win his attention, only to fail time and again. I couldn't withstand the constant rejection.

Also, I did not want him to be able to suddenly claim

me if I accomplished something in life. In my mind, I was becoming my own man and didn't need any part of him in my life. I needed a fresh start. I needed to put the past behind me, and in that moment, he was becoming a part of my past.

999 Points of Light and 1 Big Lie

To add insult to injury, around that same time, my father was recognized as an exceptional community leader, youth mentor, and role model by President George H. W. Bush. He had created a mentorship program for black youth in the Washington, D.C., metropolitan area, but none of the seven biological children he abandoned were invited to be a part. How ironic.

While giving an interview about his recognition from the president with a local TV station, my father stated: "We have 125 black fathers working within this society. You read in the newspaper so many negative things about black men, but we stand as renaissance men committed to academic excellence —committed to make a difference."

I was dumbfounded. I was speechless. I was confused. How could a man who abandoned his first family, abandoned his second family, abandoned his third family, and lived a lie with his fourth family, have the audacity to stand on the stage with the president of the United States and continue to lie before the world?

My mind could not reconcile what I was seeing. The level of arrogance and narcissism was nauseating. I knew the truth. Still, even as I had determined to leave him behind, I longed for his love and acceptance. It was a twisted set of emotions that I could not process. And in truth, as I grew into adulthood, I still lacked confidence. I was insecure. Still enraged, I didn't trust the intentions of others and struggled to foster real relationships. I was a mess. I thought if I could just distance myself from the past, I could overcome these feelings.

That proved difficult, though. As I will elaborate, you will learn how deep and twisted J.D.'s (my father's) actions went.

The Complexities of an Absent Father

Many fatherless children are now adults dealing with the effects of fatherlessness. Some of us grew up in cultures that forced us to grow up quickly, where we were told to suppress our feelings. These dysfunctional family attitudes are common across all socioeconomic and ethnic backgrounds. The effects of abandonment are often dismissed, called a myth, minimized, and overlooked. For this reason, I'm going to explain the impact of the rejection and the abandonment of my father. Let me walk you through a little bit of his story.

My father was born September 18, 1932. He was one of eight children. The family resided in the vicinity of Norfolk, Virginia, with roots in Bertie County, North Carolina.

According to family stories, his mother, Roxanna, was a strong-willed woman who ran the show. She was supposedly the boss, and my grandfather, John, seemed to be passive like my maternal grandfather, Leroy. What's interesting is that my maternal grandmother, Verdell, was strong-willed and ran the show as well. I can only imagine the effect this had on four black/brown boys growing up in the '30s and '40s. Most of the boys seemed to have similar challenges in their adulthood. In a recent conversation with my aunt, she admitted to me that many of the family stories were simply embarrassing. I will always appreciate and never forget her candor and humility about this.

J.D. was a handsome, charismatic character and a magnet for attention, according to the women who knew him. He was confident, humorous, well-spoken, and the life of the party. He was a self-described renaissance man, but he had minimal financial resources. He was most focused on protecting his false image at the expense of anyone or anything that got in his way. His most valuable asset was his gift of gab, which afforded him many opportunities, both good and bad. When he stepped into the room, the room would stop. He knew his role and exploited every aspect of it. He commonly referred to himself as a *sex machine*. That was one true statement, for sure. Because he was so good at performing, no one would suspect the other, sinister side of him.

I'll never forget the time one of my cousins shared a story about a cruel statement J.D. had made about her weight. It devastated her, and I could tell that it still impacted her more than twenty years after his death. As I reflect, this was the measure of his character. He was very shallow and image-conscious, and if you didn't look a particular way, he would reject you. To watch him in action, it would be hard to believe that this man, whom the public loved, was the man I have described.

J.D. Gets Married—for the First Time

In August of 1954, J.D. got married to his first wife. According to her, he never graduated from high school or college and went into the military to fight in the Korean War. During his time in battle, he suffered an injury in combat and lost a kidney. Based on the marriage certificate, he was married at twenty-one and began to build a life with his nineteen-year-old wife. They had four children, two girls and two boys. One of the boys had special needs and, to this day, requires twenty-four-hour care. Knowing my father, this was a major issue that did not coincide with his bigger plan.

In 1966, he took a stab at politics and ran for Norfolk City Council. He lost that race, and his life began a nasty decline. During the campaign, he had an affair with his personal assistant, and she became pregnant with a boy. In an effort to cover his tracks, he moved her to Connecticut and continued his relationship with her. They later also had a daughter. He was juggling life and two families. Shortly thereafter, he completely abandoned the first family.

His departure left them in financial ruin. They lost the family home, and a host of other issues ensued. My brother with special needs became a ward of the state. He was institutionalized, and has been ever since. Another brother began a very destructive pattern and murdered his wife. One of my sisters became pregnant as a teen and started a journey where she found herself in abusive and toxic relationships well into adulthood. Another sister had severe struggles since the moment J.D. abandoned them, and she ended up getting married and moving away. They were all teens, and their father was gone, never to return.

My older siblings shared gruesome stories about the physical and emotional abuse my father put their mother through. The abuse and abandonment led to psychiatric issues, and she was eventually institutionalized. She attempted suicide while in the institution.

The Traveling Man

J.D.'s decisions behind the scenes, rather than the lost election, started a professional, personal, and financial decline from which he would never recover. His affair with his assistant was the beginning of closed doors in many areas of his life. I'm sure the financial and emotional effects weighed on him, as his energy had to shift from his career to covering up his deeds.

By the time he met my mother, he was no longer involved with politics and instead traveled as a labor relations negotiator. This was probably the worst occupation for him, simply because he was able to travel with no accountability. Considering the fact that his lifestyle and behaviors were common for men of his generation, it is easy to see how he fell to his vices.

A Warning

As I have learned more about my father's life and poor decisions, I use this information as a warning to myself. Because I have so many of his traits and I'm in the public eye, I have to be careful of the same temptations that took him down. People in the spotlight attract the good and the bad. The appealing things may be bright and shiny, but that doesn't make them good. Knowing the difference is important. After being in the public eye for more than twenty-five years, I have learned those valuable lessons. In the early days, though, I unknowingly followed in my father's footsteps.

His Legacy of Lies

Some people have asked me if I am proud to be able to brag about my father being recognized by the president of the United States. I have mixed feelings. On one hand, I know that I am the son of a man who was recognized on the world stage for doing something positive. On the other hand, I know that much of what he was recognized for is a lie, so I have conflicting emotions. The lies do not diminish the help he offered to the students who were a part of his program, but the truth is that he had seven biological children he completely ignored. His abandonment of his children has sent shockwaves that will continue to impact many generations.

Trained to Cover Up Foolishness

Not everyone was happy when I began sharing my story about my father and the effects of his abandonment. I was surprised to get a nasty phone call from one of my siblings after a public speaking engagement where I mentioned my father's full name and showed a video clip of him with President Bush. My sibling questioned why I would share that information and told me I was wrong for doing so. In that moment, I realized how powerful my father's influence was. It was almost like a spell. This sibling suffered some of the worse emotional abuse at the hands of my father, but was now coming to his defense. I was baffled! The emotionally abusive things my father did would bring some to tears. It was at this point that I began to see the effect of covering up foolishness.

My response to my sibling was simple. I plainly stated: "This is my story about my relationship with my father, and I am going to tell the truth." I was not in the business of protecting a false legacy.

The Paternal Divorce—My New Voice

Our identity is at the core of who we are. Because of my disconnect from my father, my identity was severely damaged. He made a strong statement to me each time I reached out to him and he rejected me. His rejection said, "I don't want you, and I don't love you." Carrying his last name did not make sense. I remember asking myself, "Why am I walking around with a man's name who wants nothing to do with me?" I was helpless to change him, but I felt that I could permanently remove him from my name the same way he had removed me from his life.

I remember sitting in the parking lot across from Lenox

Mall in Atlanta, Georgia, in 1991 when I decided to legally remove his last name from my name. I'm often asked if I regret removing his name. My response is a resounding, "No!" In many ways, it gave me the opportunity to establish my own identity (outside of his influence and other forced, toxic historical influences). It was a fresh start for me. I didn't want my future children carrying his name, either. This was my *paternal divorce*, and it was final. I simply adopted my middle name as my last name, and the rest is history.

Over the years, I've spoken to many people who have felt the same way about their fathers and understand why I made that decision. I've known some people to legally adopt a stepfather's last name and remove the birth father's name for the same reasons. I'm not suggesting that anyone should do this. I am simply sharing my response to a broken identity. As I have matured, I don't have a problem using his last name on occasion, if required. I'm no longer ashamed of the name because I have so many siblings, nieces, and nephews who carry the name (even with its toxic history) and represent it well.

Similarities I Cannot Deny

Even with removing my father's last name, one of the most difficult conclusions I've had to acknowledge is that I am very much like my father. It's somewhat baffling because I didn't spend more than twenty-four hours collectively in his presence while I was growing up. Yet, from what I have been told, my gestures, vibe, and personality are almost identical to his, which bothered me for a time, because I wanted no parts of him. I was ashamed of him and embarrassed by the mess he created, and didn't want to be likened to him.

A son's identity often comes from his father. I was ashamed of my father and did not like the fact that I was so much like him. As a result, I found myself shutting down and holding back. Deep on the inside, I really just wanted my father to love me, and I knew that wasn't the case. There is nothing so destructive as knowing your father doesn't love you, and there is nothing you can do about it. I could act as if it didn't affect me, but it impacted my core and my identity. It didn't matter if my mother and grandparents loved me; I longed for my father's love, and I knew it did not exist.

In an interesting way, my father's absence did give me an identity and helped to establish convictions. Had I not experienced what I experienced, I would not have developed my unwavering conviction to help youth navigate the challenges of childhood into adulthood. I would not have developed my conviction for intolerance of fraudulent people and actions. I would not have developed the conviction to be an active and present father for my own kids and to strive to be the best dad I can possibly be. All of this came out of something negative, but the result has been positive. It makes sense to me now.

My College Dropout Years

As I said earlier, moving to Atlanta for college at the age of seventeen proved to be more than my maturity level could handle. In addition to the poor choices I made, the toxic relationship I had started in high school found its way to Georgia. The relationship was a terrible distraction and served as the catalyst for dropping out of college. I was emotionally drained and had become codependent. Saving the relationship became my primary focus until one night, when everything came to a head, her father and I clashed.

The things I said to him were profane and vicious. I felt a sense of gratification in my responses toward him, and failed to see the depth of my condition. In my mind, I thought I was winning against him, but in reality, I was losing terribly, and I was about to see how much. As I reflect, I see that the confrontations I had with this young lady's father stemmed from my issues and lack of respect for my own father. In many ways, my outbursts toward him were outbursts I wished I could have had toward my own father.

Seven Whole Days That Changed My Life

The emotions and immaturity levels of two improperly trained and dysfunctional eighteen-year-olds were a recipe for disaster. The relationship had deteriorated to the point where we were physically involved with other people while still trying to fix each other. Due to the volatile nature of the relationship, there were threats of violence from her family toward me, and from me toward her family. It was a bona fide ghetto situation in the extreme.

We finally decided to call it quits—kind of. Because of the physical and emotional connection we had, we would still find ourselves connecting sexually. It was a twisted and sick cycle of dysfunction that never seemed to end. It was clear that something drastic would need to happen in order to bring this relationship to a close. We didn't realize that something drastic was, indeed, about to happen.

Shacked Up, Boo'd Up, and Locked Up

At one point, we moved in together without the knowledge of either of our parents, as a last effort at saving the relationship. Perversely, we were trying to conceive a child in an effort to stay connected while still seeing other people. Eventually, the living arrangements failed, and we agreed to break up.

The day after we officially broke up, I invited a woman to spend the night. The next morning, we both woke up to my ex-girlfriend standing over us as we lay unclothed in the bed. I was in disbelief. How could she be in my apartment when she had returned the key upon (partially) moving out? The only way she could have obtained another key was from the rental office, which was exactly what happened. She had convinced them that she was locked out, so they gave her the spare key. Her entry into the apartment was the catalyst to an unfortunate sequence of events that would follow.

As she stood over us, I was beyond angry. I felt violated. After all, we were no longer in an official relationship, and I was free to sleep with any woman who wanted to sleep with me. Although she had some items in my apartment that she still needed to retrieve, it did not give her the right to trespass and enter the apartment without permission since her name was nowhere on the lease. This resentment festered in my mind as I was de-escalating the immediate situation. After calming down, we agreed that she would come back later that evening to get her remaining items. I could not have imagined how the night would end.

Everything was tense when she arrived. I was still livid over her violation. She was livid over seeing me in bed with another woman, which baffled me because she was in a full-blown relationship with another man. Nevertheless, our relationship was terminally ill and was in the process of its final death—kind of.

As we began to discuss the events of the day, anger took over. Before I knew it, she had thrown the key she was given by the rental company off the balcony. The next thing I knew, I was throwing her full chest of clothes off the balcony. I then discovered that she had her male friend's suede jacket in my closet. I proceeded to stuff it into the toilet. This set her off. She unleashed a flurry of punches that would have made Mike Tyson proud. Then she was throwing blows and I was throwing clothes. All of her remaining belongings ended up either over the balcony or in the hallway. I refused to hit her, though.

As things continued to deteriorate, we simultaneously called the police. Within minutes, they showed up and assessed the situation. We were both criminally responsible for what had occurred, so we were both arrested. She was arrested for her physical assault and I was arrested for destroying her property. I could not believe what was happening. How had this situation deteriorated to this level so quickly? Suddenly, I was sitting in the back of the police car and headed to jail. This was not my first brush with the law, however, and my past deeds were about to catch up with me.

As they were processing me, they discovered that I had an outstanding warrant because I had failed to pay restitution in another matter. I could not be released on bond until I could come up with the $1,100 to be released. I didn't have $1,100. Calling my father was not an option, and I dared not call my mother with this foolishness, either. I began to call everyone I knew, but it was a holiday weekend and everyone was out of town. I could not believe that I was going to be stuck in jail over the entire weekend. Reality set in.

This relationship had landed me in jail, and I could only blame myself for staying in it and allowing things to escalate to such a toxic level. At this point, I knew the relationship would never be the same. My time in jail left a lasting impression of the level of consequences attached to being involved with her.

I immediately went into survival mode as I navigated jail life. All I could think about was being raped in jail. The thought of that disgusted and terrified me. I refused to shower or sleep anywhere that was isolated. My goal was to smell as bad as possible so that I would hopefully ward off a rape attempt. I slept in the common area, sitting up on the wall. I stayed to myself for the most part, other than selling cigarettes for inmates from time to time. I thought that this would keep me on the safe side of things. I made a major mistake at one point and let one of the other inmates know that the police did not take my ID or money when I was booked. He used that information to set up an ambush.

A group of guys I felt somewhat comfortable with asked me to come into one of the private cells. I thought they wanted me to sell more cigarettes. Before I knew it, they tied a sheet around my neck and started putting their hands in my pockets. I thought they were trying to remove my pants and I began to yell at the top of my lungs, but the sheet restricted my shouts. All I could do was to grab my pants in a desperate attempt to stop my worst nightmare from happening. Suddenly, it ended as quickly as it started. They got what they wanted: the money I had mentioned to the other inmate. While I wasn't raped, I was terrified and didn't know what to do. I was afraid of another attack later if I could not figure out a way to remove myself from the environment.

In an act of desperation, I began to act as if I were having convulsions. The emergency medics were called, and I was transported to the hospital for evaluation. I must have performed pretty well because everyone at the jail thought I was dying. I thought it had worked, but the next twelve hours were about to be some of the most humiliating of my life.

The Homeless Man and the Honey Bun

I was lying handcuffed and smelly in the emergency room rolling bed, and the shame of being handcuffed to the bed where everyone could see me was unbearable. A homeless man walked up to me, gave me his stale honey bun, and told me that I looked like I needed his bun more than he did. He also told me that I did not belong in jail and that I needed to get things in order. That extension of kindness from the homeless man spoke to me on a deeper level than I had ever experienced before.

After the doctors determined that I did not need to be admitted to the hospital, I was transported to the same jail cell where I had been attacked. Because I had decided to press charges, I did not have to worry about them being around me anymore. At that point, I was focused on getting out of there. After seven whole days, my friend Kevin loaned me the $1,100. With the restitution paid, I was finally released. The other criminal charges were dropped.

I did not want to be picked up by anyone when I was released. I had not bathed in those seven days, so I was not the most pleasant-smelling person for someone to be around. I took the train home and immediately got into the shower.

It was time to make some serious decisions and to finally let this relationship go. If my time in jail taught me anything, it at least taught me that. But my heart was in too deep to end it completely. Instead, I began the process of backing away from her.

Although we never revisited a serious relationship after that, we still had sexual encounters for three more years, even though we were both sexually involved with multiple people. We had an emotional tie that ran deeper than anyone could have ever imagined. Because I did not have a father to help me navigate this area of my life, I was clueless as to what I was feeling or the impact of what I was doing. I was being led by my toxic emotions. Something had to change.

Wandering Without a Vision

I went into a deep low point after my release from jail and went unemployed for months, spending my days on a sofa watching soap operas. I lacked mental toughness and would shut down easily when things didn't go my way. The upbeat energy I used to have was now gone. I let myself go on many levels. Because I was used to manipulating myself out of bad situations, this seemed unbearable. I could not envision any escape from the hole I had dug for myself. I knew I needed a change, but how? The best thing I could figure out was to get a job.

Finally Got a Job

I finally started working as a delivery driver for a local fast-food company. I still had no real vision for my life at this point, other than wanting to perform on stage in some capacity. I was not interested in returning to the traditional college model because it seemed like a trap for me. I was a free spirit and enjoyed being free to explore and learn without the confines of a traditional classroom.

The previous year, I had been very active in the music scene and was the main keyboard player for a local band. I was able to connect with them again, and that filled some of the idle time in my life.

Later that year, my friend Sergio approached me with an opportunity to join him in recruiting for *Showtime at the Apollo*. It was almost like a dream come true because I was merely wandering through life at that point. I accepted the offer, and we began to start passing out flyers for auditions at a local nightclub. We promoted day and night, and the auditions were a tremendous success.

Party Man!

After the success of the *Showtime at the Apollo* auditions, I decided to take a shot at promoting club events. My first event sold, out and my new life as a concert and party promoter began. This was the worst environment I could find myself in, though, because it was a breeding ground for my out-of-control behavior. I was being promoted on the radio, and my events attracted thousands of people. With that came endless opportunities for sexual encounters. I was truly my father's son, which became apparent very quickly.

The Cycle Continues

After rebounding some, the lifestyle I was living was still reckless, promiscuous, and dangerous. I had no sexual integrity. It was the one thing I found that I could do with ease. Using protection regularly was not one of my preferred practices. In a sick way, I got a thrill out of dodging the pregnancy or disease bullet. It wasn't until I contracted gonorrhea that I started to take such things a bit more seriously. Fortunately, or perhaps unfortunately, gonorrhea was curable. Because I did not feel the real impact of my lifestyle, even this did nothing to stop my reckless behavior.

I was addicted to my sexual conquests and found victory in targeting women and gaining their consent. I knew whom to target. If a woman had a scent of rejection, insecurity, or need for validation, I could tap into that instantly. I would target women to see how quickly I could have a sexual encounter with them. Sometimes the encounters would be the same day, while others would take a couple of weeks. Many of the women were dealing with the same issues I was dealing with, and we would find comfort in the familiarity. Again, it was a very empty place. For me, there was rarely any emotionally intimate connection. These relationships were purely selfish and exploitative. I didn't care if the women were eight-months pregnant by another man, not the most attractive, or known for being easy—I needed my fix. My life revolved around these conquests.

But even with that, I knew I was empty. I knew there was more to life than what I was doing, but I didn't know how to get there. Sex had become my drug of choice. I became a master of it, and it served as the one of the biggest distractions of my life.

Ironically, I would not sleep with the women whom I was really fond of. It was as if I subconsciously did not want to taint them. Even if they threw themselves at me, I would not cross that line. It was weird, but I can only attribute it to having respect for them. Perhaps I was learning, without knowing it, how to respect people.

Guess Who Is Going to Be a Daddy?

In 1993, I learned I was to become a father. The mother of my child didn't want to have the baby; she wanted an abortion due to aggressive pressure from her family. This hit me really hard for some reason. Perhaps the fact that I had paid for an abortion for another young lady a couple of months prior impacted my new conviction. For the first time in my life, I felt strongly about right and wrong. But the choice was hers and out of my control. I didn't know what to do, so for the first time in my life, I prayed. I mean, *really* prayed.

I made her a promise. If she kept the baby, I would become a man. I would grow up. I would be the father that the baby needed. I wanted this baby more than anything in the world. I was scared, but I was steadfast.

I knew it was time for me to grow up and take responsibility for this unborn child. This was my first step in becoming a man and the beginnings of a foundation that would become a major platform in my life.

My Special Gift Arrives

My daughter was born on a cold winter's day in

February of 1994. I felt incapable, untrained, and alone, but I had to continue to man up. She brought out the best in me, the desire to change, and the motivation to get my life together. She brought about these things in me before she was even born. I didn't know what I was doing, but I knew I had to keep going. I refused to become to her what my father had become to me. I was going to be present and involved in her life.

And so my life began to change. My little girl helped me to become a better man very slowly, day by day.

While I was being inspired to become a good dad, I was still struggling in other areas. My relationship with my daughter's mother had taken a downturn. We never had an emotionally intimate connection, and I quickly became dissatisfied with the situation. My reckless sexual behaviors continued, as I established multiple other relationships. I smoked weed every night in order to cope with my unhappiness. I was miserable, and it was my own fault, but I didn't know how to get out of it without risking losing my daughter in a custody battle. Fortunately, when the relationship did eventually fall apart, we were awarded joint custody.

The Gut Punch I Didn't See Coming—
J.D. Dies

Soon after my daughter's birth, I received word that my dad had died after a short battle with colon cancer. The news hit me like a ton of bricks. I found out when my mother handed me the newspaper and I saw his quarter-page obituary, front and center. The most surreal feeling overcame me. After reading the half-true obituary, I remember exclaiming, "That's what you get, you ___!" And then I immediately broke down. It was like PTSD. I had so many unanswered questions, so many thoughts and memories that would never ever get closure. I was grieving and celebrating at the same time. In one breath, I was crying, and then the next, I was feeling as if he'd finally gotten what he deserved.

My father's death brought a very profound realization. It ended a reign of control and lies that had affected not only my life, but also the lives of my six older siblings. He did everything in his power to hide us from each other, but he could no longer prevent us from learning the awful truth.

I still could not understand how he could be celebrated by the president of the United States, politicians, and pastors as being an upstanding father and community leader when he rejected seven of his children. There were those who knew the truth but opted to cover it up at the expense of those same children. There were even people who said that I should boast about the fact that my father was celebrated by the president. As I shared before, there was no way I could do that, because the celebration was based on lies. If the complete story had been told, he would not have been honored in that way. But it was becoming painfully clear that his choices would have generational ramifications, which had to be addressed.

All of my father's children have suffered from his choices. He went to his grave refusing to fully acknowledge the truth. His lies continued even into his funeral program. Although he had eleven children—that I know of—only his four youngest children were listed in the program, which added more insult to my injury.

Even in death, he was able to hurt me. Though he knew he was dying, he never reached out to me. It devastated and angered me to know that he was content with going to his grave leaving things as they were.

Memories

The memories started to rush in. I remembered one

phone call in which he had acknowledged that he had failed as a father and promised to do better, yet he continued with the same pattern. I realized that I would forever be left with memories like these and would never receive the answers.

J.D. knew I was his child. The court-ordered blood test and tens of thousands of dollars in garnished child support payments proved that. His silence as he closed his chapter on earth was just one more slap in the face. Ironically, my father never knew I had removed his last name.

My father's death further orphaned me, though I thought of myself as already divorced from him. Death is permanent, with no second chances to get things right. As I was still searching for an identity as a man and a young father, there was now not even a glimmer hope of any relationship with my own father. Though I had started on the right path, the snares and traps were still thick, and now the most important avenue of reconciliation was closed.

At this point, I knew I needed to look deeper into myself and the issues that had plagued me for my entire life. I had to come to terms with the fact that my father would never apologize or say, "I love you." I grieved what never was and what never was to be, which spiraled me into a dark spiritual place.

Wasted Potential

My father had so much potential, but his internal issues cut short his ability to realize it. His fifteen minutes of fame with the senior President Bush was the height of his life, but he could have done so much more. At the time of his death, J.D., his fourth wife, and their four children were living in a three-bedroom, lower-middle-class apartment. He portrayed a completely different image than the reality of his situation. If it weren't for a financial settlement after his death, due to an initial misdiagnosis of his cancer, he would have left his last family in the same financial ruin as he did his first family. A person's financial positioning does not speak to their personal worth, but sometimes a person's integrity does impact his or her financial situation, which I believe was the case with my father.

All of this was a life lesson that resonated with me, because again, I have so many of his personality traits. As a teen and young adult, I had already followed in J.D.'s negative footsteps, and though I was making changes, I knew there needed to be more.

The Truth Versus His "Truth"

As I have shared, my father did everything in his power to hide the truth. The amount of energy he spent trying to cover his tracks and ignore the truth of his past had to weigh on him daily. He could not ignore it entirely, though. He was required to pay my mother $625 in child support each month until the day he died. J.D. was used to sweeping the truth under the rug, but I salute my mother for holding him accountable for his actions, or inactions. This was probably the first time in his life he had been forced to take responsibility. Because he was so clever and persuasive with his words, he could talk himself out of just about anything with just about anyone, except the judge who awarded my mother child support in arrears.

All of J.D.'s abandoned children were severely impacted by his absence and emotional abuse. There are a couple of his children who see him in a very positive light, and I respect that. That is all they knew, and none of our collective experiences will change their experiences with him. But it doesn't change the fact that *his truth* was, for the most part, very different from *the truth*.

My father never walked any of his daughters down the

aisle at their wedding. He never saw any of his children graduate from college. He missed so much because he was living a lie. I did not want that for my life. I wanted to be authentic. Observing the end result of my father's life hit me hard and began to shape my personal philosophy. I know that it was also a warning to me. I heard it loud and clear and did not want my legacy to repeat the same cycle of dysfunction and destruction that my father left behind.

Breaking the Cycle

My relationship with my siblings is positive. I was able to gather nine of my father's eleven children for the first time. It was a nice meeting, but a little awkward. One set of children had glowing accounts of a man who had helped so many, while another set of his children had stories to the contrary. There was one set of children quietly questioning and doubting the paternity of these strangers who claimed to be their siblings, while those other children knew their paternity and the full truth about J.D. Overall, the event went well, but I could feel the influence of his spirit still around. I couldn't help but think to myself, "Why would someone want to claim this broke, narcissistic, deadbeat as their father if it weren't true?"

Over the years, I have learned to respect my siblings' relationships, or lack thereof, with our father. With that said, not every sibling was open to being a part of the reunion, especially one in particular. I view her response as indicative of my father's presence. I actually met her in 2005 when I went to visit her, and she was very nice, kind, and welcoming, but as of today, she has stopped communicating. I'm sure it goes back to a wound my father left behind. Instead, I focus on establishing relationships with the siblings who want to be in a relationship.

My ultimate goal is to try to help the next generation overcome the dysfunction and sadness of my father's legacy. My nieces and nephews have faced their own challenges—a wide-reaching impact of my father's treatment of my siblings. I can see the results clearly. It hurts me on so many levels because they don't understand the real impact of his absence and how it affected their parents.

The Positive Legacy

Although I have shared many negative aspects about my father, I would be disingenuous if I did not share some of the things I did admire about him. Regardless of how he treated me, he was still my father, so I will always long for his love, whether I ever received it or not.

I can hold on to the few positive memories I did share with him. I will never forget when he bought me a bike and brought it to me. I will also never forget when he bought me a pair of shoes and left them for me to pick up at the Foot Locker shoe store. I remember getting to eat lunch with him at McDonald's. And I hold on to the memory of him finally inviting me into his home to sit and talk with one of my younger brothers.

I admire the confidence he had and his ability to build a life with limited education. His negotiation skills were remarkable. For all his faults, there were these positives. Perhaps this is what the other set of siblings saw: all of the good. To some extent, maybe the rest of us were blinded by his unwillingness to stick around.

A Wild, Sex-Filled Church Conference

No one knew what I was dealing with after my father's death. I'm sure most people assumed that I was indifferent, but that was far from the truth. I was lost and searching for answers I would never receive. It was a very uncomfortable space to be in.

While still dealing with my father's recent passing, I attended a conference that was labeled as a church conference. For years, my younger cousins had talked about a mid-winter church conference they always attended. They did not talk about it because of the spiritual impact it had on their lives, but rather because of the wild sexual escapades that occurred there. Part of me felt as though they were exaggerating because my mind could not reconcile wild sexual escapades and a church conference. As a result of my skepticism, they strongly encouraged me to attend one of the conferences to see for myself.

Upon arriving at the conference, it did not take me long to realize they had been telling me the truth. Within two hours, I found myself in a hotel room about to have sex with one of the women from the conference. My mind was in shock. It would have been easy, but I did not have sex with her. I knew this was not supposed to be happening at a church conference. Unfortunately, though, it was the culture of the conference, and it ran rampant. The level of sexual indiscretions that occurred among the teens and young adults was mind-boggling to me, and it triggered a shift in my heart.

When I saw a fourteen-year-old girl going from room to room to have sex, I could not help but think about my daughter. This young girl was someone's daughter, and I was sure her parents did not send her to the church conference to have sex.

On the last night of the conference, there was a guest speaker who called out everything that was going on. It was as if he was reading my mind. He spoke about the wild sexual indiscretions, but he also talked about the severe consequences that could happen as a result. His message was something I had never heard in church. It was compelling. It was inspiring. It moved me to take a step in what I felt was the right direction.

On that cold night in December 1994, at the wild, sex-filled church conference in Baltimore, I knew it was time for a change. As a result, I accepted the speaker's invitation to receive Christ into my life. I was not fully aware of what my new commitment would require of me and of the journey I was about to embark upon, but I knew it was time for a change. I was tired of how I was living, and I was ready for things to be different.

This was a decision that no one had to convince or scare me into making. I didn't know where else to turn because my life was at the bottom. I knew I was not where I was supposed to be. I knew that there was a greater purpose for my life and my choices were causing me to miss it. At that point, the overhaul of my life began.

Don't be fooled. There was a fear of the unknown and a longing to go back to my old, familiar ways. Temptation didn't just go away. But I was tired of being empty and of attracting and being attracted to other empty people. I was tired of the results of my choices, and it was time to grow up.

The Church Dynamic

Let me be clear, I did not grow up going to church, and I am not writing this book in an attempt to get you to go to church. Not that attending a healthy, legitimate church is a bad thing, but what matters most is much deeper than that.

Much of what I had seen in church turned me off. The hypocrisy, the money games, the manipulations, the false images of what was supposed to be the Messiah, the historical and biblical omissions, the sexual indiscretions, and the cliques—they all repelled me. For years, I didn't see the point of going to church just to live the same way I was living outside of the church. The transformation that occurred in my life was much more profound than the institution and system of church. I had changed in fundamental ways. And while I am thankful for that, it was my father's death—and even his life—that set me on the path toward transformation.

How Fatherlessness Nearly Cost Me My Marriage

I never considered how the lack of a father would affect my romantic relationships and, ultimately, my marriage. It makes sense, though. My father was absent and a poor example of how a man should conduct himself in a marriage.

Marriage was not something that I ever thought I would do. My stance was that one woman could never satisfy me. My sexual history had exposed me to a lot of escapades, and I had not been able to see myself with only one woman. My heart was changing, along with my mind and my appetite. Slowly but surely, my old life was becoming unattractive, and the new life that was being revealed to me was becoming my personal focus.

One day when I was working at the radio station, a woman named Trish (Latricia) called and requested a song. She had a bubbly, energetic personality that made me want to meet her. The radio station was sponsoring an outdoor concert the next day, so I invited her to come check it out. To my surprise, she did. When she introduced herself to me, I could sense there was something different. I was instantly attracted to her, but not for the same reasons I was attracted to women in the past. She was mature and assertive. She was someone I felt I could build something with—and I ascertained all of this from only the first meeting.

From that day, I was determined to reconnect with her. I would send her shout-outs over the air, and she would call me in the studio. However, getting back together proved difficult. I would invite her to events, but she would refuse to go. I had rarely been turned down for dates, but she didn't deter me. Trish was steadfast and unmovable, but in true J.D. fashion, I was persistent.

One day she called me and asked if I wanted to go to an event with her. I was excited out of my mind, until I learned where she wanted to go—church. Although I was trying to walk on a better path, I was not sold on the idea of regular church attendance yet. Only reluctantly did I agree to attend the launch of the new church she was about to become a part of.

When the day arrived, I was nervous but knew that if I had any chance at getting to know her more, I needed to attend this event. I didn't know what to expect when I stepped into the small, multipurpose room. Was this going to be one of those weird church events? Were they going to take four offerings? I didn't know.

Trish came over and sat with me shortly after I took my seat. Sitting so close to her, I could feel the butterflies in my stomach. I played it cool. I'm sure she had no clue what was going on with me. But there was something going on. This was the moment I knew there was something more to what I was feeling. Although I was attracted to her, there was no sexual desire at all. I just wanted to get to know her. This was a first!

As the church service began, I tolerated the praise and worship. It was rough on the ears, but there was a genuineness that I was not used to seeing in a church environment. As the pastor began to speak, I realized he was the same person who had called everything out at the wild, sex-filled church conference I had attended in Baltimore shortly after my father's death. I was floored that I had been given this full-circle experience, and from that day forward, I was hooked.

You might think that Trish and I hit it off and started dating immediately. On the contrary, we actually backed away from each other. She was dealing with her own set of issues, and I was really in no position to be in another relationship. I needed to mature more, and I didn't need any distractions. With our budding relationship on ice, we both focused on our own challenges, knowing things would work out if they were meant to. As it turned out, they did—kind of.

After nearly a year of independent self-focus, we decided to pursue a relationship. This is when the gloves came off and we both discovered we still had more internal work to do. Trish was strong-willed and independent, much like all of the women in my life who had raised or instructed me. This clashed with my strong-willed, passive-aggressive personality. Our first official date was filled with arguments and power struggles simply over who controlled the radio. After that date, I vowed to never call her again.

Once again, I was facing another major life decision without the guidance of a father. I had no reference point to pull from, no fatherly relationship advice to recall. It was a conversation with my friend Kenny that made me reconsider my future with Trish, and he helped talk me back from the edge of calling it quits. Kenny reminded me why I had chosen Trish in the first place. He also reminded me that that this was a part of the process I would go through with just about anyone, and he pointed out my prideful attitude.

After that conversation with Kenny, I decided to see if Trish wanted to continue pursuing our relationship. She agreed, and we began the process of working through our issues. After several months of dating and with the permission of the pastor (how crazy does that sound?), I asked Trish to marry me. She said yes!

The severity of our issues was not apparent until after we got engaged. Although we did not have sex before we got married, our relationship became very physically intimate, which clouded our judgment about our other hidden issues. Some of our previous toxic patterns started to come to the surface, and we didn't know what to do about them. Things finally deteriorated to a very low point and, with invitations already mailed, I called off the wedding just weeks before. I believe that may have been the wakeup call Trish needed. After she promised to work on her critical issues, I agreed to move forward with the wedding.

However, even this proved to be a bad thing. During this time, I was able to hide my darkest areas because I was focusing on her. In my arrogance and immaturity, I felt vindicated, as if I had somehow won the battle. My line of thinking would prove to be detrimental in married life, and it would be years before I worked through it.

As I approached my wedding day, the fact that all of my previous relationships had failed did not cross my mind. I was focused on getting through the actual wedding and getting to the wedding night festivities. Though we were fully aware of the warning signs before the wedding, we moved forward anyway. It was clear to everyone except us that this new marriage would face major challenges.

The marriage was incredibly dysfunctional and toxic from the onset. Shortly after the wedding, my dark side came out and my behaviors began to resemble my teenage behaviors with my mother. There were countless crisis marriage-counseling sessions with various advisors and counselors. There were nasty emails and text messages, with neither person being willing to back down. My responses to marital disagreements became volatile and destructive. While my wife and I never were physically abusive toward one another, there were profane verbal assaults, destruction of property, and emotional withdrawals that reflected our severe relational deficiencies and immaturity. These confrontations caused severe damage in the relationship that took many years to heal.

My attitude was selfish and prideful. Instead of apologizing or admitting where I was wrong, I would dig in and attempt to refocus on my wife's faults, which would lead to arguments that lasted days. We had periods of not speaking to one another that would last months at a time. It was miserable—but for some odd reason, I refused to give up.

In the middle of the madness, we somehow became a family of five, with the addition of our three sons. Needless to say, the entire marriage wasn't miserable. When times were good, they were really good. When times were bad, they were really bad. That was the dynamic of the relationship at that time.

We recently celebrated our twenty-first wedding anniversary. Now that you understand the context of the beginning of our journey, you can see how powerful reaching this milestone really was. It was not an easy journey, and both of us had to relearn new habits and ways of communicating effectively. Some of these new skills were learned as a result of counseling.

Although I initially resisted counseling and didn't want others knowing my personal business, I found that counseling sessions helped me understand the root cause of many of my anger issues. My father's absence and rejections, along with anger I still had toward my mother, were all underlying problems that influenced my mindset and subsequent actions.

In order for things to change, my responses needed to change. These were choices I would have to make, and I could not blame my parents' actions or inactions for my choices. Taking responsibility for my life and my future was up to me. Understanding the impact this would have on my children was another reality I needed to come to terms with. Did I want to set a new standard, or did I want to pass down the same dysfunctions that were passed to me?

I had embraced a toxic mindset for all of my life, so change was not easy. It once again required being honest and allowing people to tell me the truth about myself. This was a painful and difficult process that I wanted to avoid, but couldn't.

Anyone who truly wants to change dysfunctional behaviors has to decide to take action. Coming face to face with internal issues can be difficult, but it can be equally liberating. Sometimes we can become so comfortable with dysfunction that we assume it's healthy and normal. As a result, we don't seek to change it. This is how many unhealthy behaviors are passed down for generations.

It took many years, a lot of tears and emotions, and a wife who was willing to address her issues as I was addressing mine. Both my wife and I knew we had our own problems to navigate, and we were both willing to do so. Because we were both committed to becoming game changers for ourselves and for our children, the ship changed course, slowly but surely.

I share this because proper fathering can play a major role in the health of our children. Fathers can be a stabilizing force to provide confidence and reassurance. Fathers can also set an example of how to conduct oneself or what type of treatment to accept. Daughters who have healthy relationships with their fathers or father figures have a positive reference point when it comes to how a man should treat a woman. Sons who have this same example are taught how to treat women properly.

The same principle applies to mothers, regarding the importance of the example they set for their sons and daughters. If a mother tolerates toxic or abusive romantic relationships in the presence of her children, it could have a severe impact on her kids' view of relationships. They will often see the acceptance of toxic or abusive behavior as normal. I strongly encourage men and women to examine the history of their romantic relationships to see if there are any toxic patterns.

A mother has the ability to provide a different kind of stability apart from a father. On an emotional level, a mother cannot do a father's job, and he cannot do hers. This is a very different role than providing financial support. In this era of increased single parenting, understanding the difference between providing financial support and emotional support is crucial. This is another reason why it's important for us to do our respective individual jobs as parents well.

Stuck in the Middle

Many of us grew up in what I call a *power-struggle culture*, in which one parent leverages time or resources for the sake of control or revenge. Typically in these situations, if one parent feels offended, violated, abused, or cheated in some capacity, their energy moves toward the offense and away from the children. Frequently, these offenses have nothing to do with the children, yet they find themselves stuck in the middle of divorce or custody battles.

If you find yourself in one of these difficult situations, please do not allow the offense that occurred in the relationship to destroy the relationship of the child with the other parent—unless, of course, there was some sort of violation or abuse toward the child. Using the child as leverage does not benefit him or her. Resist the temptation to speak negatively about the other parent in the presence of the child. With all of the financial hardship my father's abandonment caused my mother, she never spoke negatively about him. She allowed me to come to my own conclusions without injecting her emotions and opinions into the situation. She never prevented me from seeing or talking to my father. His actions were the primary influence on my impression of him.

"Fatherless" Children

The reality is that having a father in the home doesn't automatically mean the father is raising his children properly or being a positive influence. My grandfather comes to mind. Over the years, I have met with many fathers who understood that they lacked fathering skills because of how they were fathered. Additionally, I have met with many children who conveyed that they didn't get to experience the benefits of being fathered, though they had a father in the home.

Proper fathering requires focus and attention. When I use the term *proper,* I am referring to establishing a healthy parenting relationship that encourages a strong identity, confidence, and character. Proper fathering also encourages healthy lifestyle habits and disciplines pertaining to mental, physical, and financial health. Many fathers have either been improperly trained in these areas or have no training at all. For the father who wants to change this narrative, it will take some intentional work and investment, but the reward will be priceless.

If you are a child of a father who was present but absent, it is important for you to understand the dynamics of your father's life. Understanding the fact that many fathers simply do not have the tools to father properly allows for individual and family healing to occur. I have learned that dwelling on what wasn't given does not change anything. Instead, I learned from my father's shortcomings and used them as a reference point to improve my own parenting style.

Paternal Predators and Their Prey

Many people who deal with absent fathers, or absent-but-present fathers, find themselves seeking father figures. I see now that I subconsciously sought father figures to replace my father. When a male figure took interest in mentoring or coaching me, I remember thinking how I wished he might adopt me. It was a subtle and recurring thought that ended up being a major deficiency in my life.

This can create a ripe atmosphere for emotional and physical abuses. I call them *paternal predators*. These types of people understand the psychology of the fatherless and seek to exploit their deficiencies by assuming a paternal role in the lives of their victims. This can happen in gangs, schools, support groups, and any place where this deficiency is present. Many religious environments are the perfect breeding ground for paternal predators to identify and exploit their prey.

As I shared previously, I began consistently attending church starting shortly after my father's death. Coming to terms with the fact that my father was gone, and I would never get my questions answered, was a tough pill to swallow. My church had what appeared to be strong male leaders who would refer to us as spiritual sons. Initially, being referred to as a *son* was affirming, comforting, and reassuring. Eventually, it became extremely toxic and nearly destroyed me emotionally and spiritually. What I experienced in multiple church environments is something all fatherless (or motherless) men and women should be aware of.

Because I was not fully aware of my deficiencies and how paternal predators can lurk in supposed safe places, I put my guard down. I found myself competing for these paternal figures' attention by being willing to become overly sacrificial. Seeking the praise and recognition of these father figures replaced a healthy, balanced relationship. Many times, I found myself behaving and thinking like a nine-year-old child. If I ever felt rejection from a spiritual father figure, I would act out, shut down, and withdraw, just like a child.

I saw things that were emotionally abusive and unethical, and instead of speaking up, I stayed silent. Fear of being reprimanded, rejected, or publicly humiliated kept me quiet. After years of being in this environment, I wanted to leave but was afraid to, so I stayed until it was unbearable. It did not change how the Scriptures affected me or my relationship with God, but it severely impacted my faith in the church and the various religious systems that have evolved throughout history. At times, Scripture and my relationship with God were all I had to get me through those dark days.

The levels of psychological and emotional abuses I witnessed toward myself and others shook me to my core. To see grown men reduced to behaving like little boys is something I will never forget. I'm embarrassed to say that we would chase the approval of a supposed spiritual leader at the expense of our families, dreams, and relationship with God. I reached my tipping point after seeing families fall apart because one spouse was more loyal to a spiritual leader than to the other spouse. And I witnessed families falling apart because one family member was so busy working for the church that he or she neglected responsibilities at home. I realized that this was not an environment conducive for growth, and it violated much of what the Scriptures said.

Leaving that environment was very difficult. These people had become my new family, so I thought. When I left, I quickly discovered that they weren't my family and I had now become the enemy for leaving. It's ironic because as I dealt with their rejections, I was reminded that I had behaved the exact same way whenever someone else left the "church." If one of the leaders told us not to associate with someone who had left, we obeyed. Realizing this was a gut check that hit me hard. As a result, I reached out to apologize to many people I had rejected and ostracized over the years. It was humbling, but it was also a pivotal moment in my growth as a man and as a father.

Just as I was beginning to see my biological father's deficiencies, I was now able to see the same issues in these spiritual fathers, who excused their own abuses as simply being human or having character flaws but never seemed to make a genuine effort to change. I found it interesting that they would preach about the need to change but would themselves remain the same or get worse.

Internal Conflicts

It was difficult to process what had occurred because there were lots of positive experiences with the church, too. How could something be so beneficial yet so toxic at the same time? It was a recurring question to which I didn't get an answer until many years later.

The answer was consistent with human nature. While many of us have tremendous abilities to help and uplift others, we also have the ability to destroy and abuse others at the same time. Many institutional systems are operated by people who are just as flawed and wounded, if not more so, than the people who follow them. The motivation and healthy accountability level of the leaders can determine which side of their personality—helpful or harmful—will be the dominant influence in the organization.

Aftershock

For a time, I was angry with God because I didn't un-derstand why I had to deal with my father's rejection and also have to deal with the same type of rejection from so-called spiritual fathers. It was hard for me to reconcile, and it destroyed my faith in black father figures (espe-cially in religious settings). The journey was becoming long and difficult. At the same time, I was developing my own paternal convictions. Seeing how mentally depraved these spiritual leaders and their followers were challenged me to become a better father and man.

No one likes trauma. Oftentimes trauma can lead to a lifetime of internal damage and residual harm that affects others. But it doesn't have to. I was determined not to allow that to be my story. It took more than ten years to truly heal from that situation, but I learned some things in the process. My biggest takeaway was never to allow someone to hold a place of abusive authority in my life. I don't allow anyone to refer to me as their *spiritual son* and I don't, in turn, refer to myself as anyone's *spiritual father*. I mentor many people, but that is the extent of it. We have a healthy relationship that promotes mutual respect. I also have healthy mentors who respect me as a man and don't see themselves as a father figure to me. This is a personal conviction of mine, and I'm not telling you not to use those terms, but I am warning you to be careful. Be sure that you are not in a spiritually abusive relationship, even if it feels good at the moment.

I am thankful for the experience because it taught me how to trust, and it also revealed areas where I still needed to mature. It forced me out of my comfort zone and took me to a place of humility that I didn't know existed. I'm now able to use the wisdom and insight I gained to help others recover from traumatic situations.

I was eventually able to forgive and reconcile with many of the people who were a part of those toxic religious systems. The relationships are very different now. They are abuse-free and healthy. While I will never be a part of those systems again, I have learned how to appreciate people when they endeavor to have healthy relationships.

A Healthy Male Figure

Shortly after my toxic church experiences, I met a pastor in Savannah, Georgia, who was the complete opposite of what I had encountered previously. He was mild-mannered, sophisticated, and respectful. He was the pastor of a megachurch, and I was happy that he didn't approach me wanting anything. I suspect he could sense that I was severely wounded and didn't want to trigger any church PTSD.

I was guarded and approached the relationship cautiously. Over time, he proved to be trustworthy. He and his wife helped guide my wife and me through some of the most challenging times of our marriage. The timing of his introduction into my life was perfect. I needed a mentor to model being a father, and that is exactly what he did.

Through his interactions with his own children, in the way he spoke to them and empowered them, he demonstrated how to be an emotionally healthy father. He showed me a different side of fathering that I had never seen. He was secure and confident, and his children were a reflection of his parenting. I liked that our relationship wasn't one-sided. When faced with family challenges, he didn't hide them from me, and he even sought my advice on numerous occasions. It was, and is, a healthy relationship, and I'm forever thankful for his introduction into my life.

We Can Do Better

What is your story? What are the childhood disappointments that have shaped you? What positive and negative elements have you been exposed to? What lies do you believe, and how are you using those lies as an excuse to continue with dysfunctional behaviors?

There is a popular idea encouraging us to *acknowledge our truth*. As I have matured, I have come to the conclusion that at different times in my life *my* truth was not *the* truth. Once I began to desire *the* truth, my healing began. Most of us face baggage from childhood that has affected us negatively as adults. We all have moments in which we come face to face with our issues. In those moments, we can either choose to allow them to become part of who we are, or we can root them out and learn new habits and mindsets that bring freedom.

I am proof that you can retrain your mind and make an impact on your children. Even if you have let many years go by without being the parent you need to be, there is still hope. You may have a long way to go. You may have habits and mindsets that need complete rearranging. You may be a parent like my father—absent and detached. But there is hope. You can learn a new way, and you can turn the tide.

Let's unpack everything I've learned about taking ownership of my situation and turning my ugly past into a bright future. I'm going to lead you down the path of how to become a great parent, and you're going to do a lot of work on yourself in the process. In the end, you'll have the tools you need to parent your children, but you'll also have everything you need to become a better person.

The rest of this book will present to you my six lessons for becoming a better parent. There's nothing magical about them, but they work. Put in the time and effort, starting today. You'll be amazed at what will follow.

LESSON ONE

Give Your Child an Identity

Proverbs 1:1–8 and Proverbs 1:22

I remember the first time I really looked at the book of Proverbs. I was very unfamiliar with the Bible, but I felt connected to Proverbs somehow. I felt that even if I didn't understand the Bible as a whole, I could understand Proverbs.

Proverbs 1:8 hit me hard: "My child, listen when your father corrects you. Don't neglect your mother's instruction."

I didn't have a father to correct me, and my mother was preoccupied and lacked knowledge about raising a boy. I was missing two crucial life components. What was I to do? Was I doomed to be a failure? Was I headed down the path that is portrayed later in the passage—the path of being a thief, headed to the grave (Proverbs 1:13–19)?

Because my natural father was no longer alive, I knew I needed guidance, but I didn't know where to turn. Everything I tried failed until I started reading the commonsense principles in Scripture.

I remember going back to Proverbs 1:22 and reading about how "fools hate knowledge." I certainly didn't want to be a fool, but my choices up to that point in my life were, indeed, foolish. It felt as if the words on the pages were speaking directly to me. I could connect different choices I made to what the Scriptures were saying. It was liberating, and I started to understand what my issues were on a deeper level. While there was nothing I could do about the fact that I had no father and an overworked mother, that didn't mean I had to be a fool. I could choose knowledge.

My transformation started with reading Proverbs. Regardless of your religious affiliation, faith, or lack thereof, you can benefit from the commonsense wisdom in Proverbs. You might not have had a father or mother to guide you. You might have had both parents in the home yet still absent from your life. You might have struggled to navigate this world, and now, you might face the daunting task of raising your own children without having a well of parental wisdom from which to draw. You might wonder how you can possibly be a good parent when you've never had parenting modeled for you, but I'm here to tell you that it's possible.

Roots of Identity

The key to this step is first establishing *your* identity so that you can properly guide your children into finding *their* identities. This will more than likely require you to confront any issues that might still be unaddressed. I had to begin the process of establishing my identity as a man before I could instill identity into my children. Addressing my deeply rooted issues—insecurities, anger, rejection, and abandonment—was essential to my parental success. Healing often requires professional therapy, as it did in my case. I could not worry about the stigma of seeking therapy that is prevalent in many communities. I knew I needed help, so I got it.

The Demonization of African Identity

Growing up, anything pertaining to Africa normally came with a negative connotation. I was discouraged from ever visiting because late night infomercials and news reports told me that everyone was sick and impoverished, or else a criminal, cannibal, or otherwise unsavory person. All of Africa was lumped together as an uncivilized, war-torn mess, rather than a continent with fifty-four countries and more than three thousand different ethnic groups and languages.

I was never taught that Africa has some of the most beautiful beaches and landscapes in the world. I was never taught that European and Arab colonization was the reason why parts of Africa suffered from poverty and various social challenges. As a result of all of the misinformation about the continent, I had absolutely no interest or desire to go—but that was all by design.

Sadly, most of our American educational, religious, and cultural systems promote the African diaspora (or "Black History") as starting with slavery. When people who are "descendants of slavery," whether African or Hebrew, only view their history through this skewed lens, there is a danger of disassociating with who they truly are. Anyone who looked like me was typically depicted as being in some form of bondage. Whether they were in shackles and chains, handcuffs, imprisoned, addicted to a substance, or mentally oppressed, the people I most identified with faced struggle and trauma. This was projected as the norm and the status quo. Unfortunately, this narrative was created by those who sought to exploit the knowledge, skill, and labor of the unsuspecting. As I began to learn more, my eyes were opened to a diabolical system of abuse that is alive and active on multiple levels to this day.

Only once I began to learn about those Africans kings

and queens from whom (I was told) I was descended could I begin to embrace the story of African identity in its full context. The previously untaught history opened my eyes in a way that shattered the dysfunctional thoughts and belief systems that had plagued me throughout my life so far.

An important aspect of confronting my identity issues was determining where they came from. Where did my view of myself come from? Where did this subconscious dislike of "self" come from? Where did my mindset come from? I found that my identity issues were the same issues passed down through my immediate family and culture. These issues could be traced back to the slave dungeons in West Africa. While many people will dismiss the impact the Middle Passage still has today, I needed to rule it out as an influence in my life. What I discovered on a trip to the slave dungeons in West Africa shocked me to my core and helped me to understand the depth of what occurred, as well as its residual impact centuries later.

For those descended from the victims of one of the most horrific episodes in human history—the transatlantic slave trade—understanding the identity theft that occurred may offer more context to our lives. From the moment an enslaved mother, father, son, daughter, doctor, leader, teacher, etc., entered one of the dungeons that were spread out over West and East Africa, there was an intentional effort to erase that person's identity. Religion, a lack of education, and physical and psychological abuse were all tactics used to disrupt the natural flow of these people's lives.

I can only imagine the abuses and manipulations my ancestors endured upon arriving in America. I can only imagine how having their names changed multiple times when they were sold to a new plantation affected them. I can only imagine the emotional trauma they faced, never having an opportunity to sort through. I can only imagine the impact of the numerous rapes, beatings, and humiliations they endured. I can only imagine the impact of the fatherlessness that came from the constant rape of the enslaved women, some of whom would give birth to more than twenty children in their lives. I can only imagine the names they were called that destroyed any hope for a positive identity.

I am a descendant of the strongest of the strong who endured the Middle Passage. I am also a descendant of theft, lies, and physical, psychological, and spiritual abuse. How could this possibly impact me over 150 years removed from the most intense years of American slavery?

Generations of abuse do not simply disappear. The effects last for generations more. By no means should what happened during slavery be used as an excuse for poor behavior, but the abuse and trauma should not be dismissed from the conversation. Understanding its impact can be one of the first steps to changing the narrative for present and future generations.

Many addictions can be linked to how my ancestors coped with the treatment they endured. Alcoholism, drug abuse, sexual abuse, physical abuse, overeating, and emotional dysfunctions are all problems passed down to relatives on both sides of my family. While many cultures face these same challenges, I have noticed the negative impact of slavery on my family firsthand. For me to ignore how this impacted my identity would be irresponsible. While I may never know the individual stories, I can see results throughout my family that speak volumes to the level of trauma that occurred.

Coming to terms with these facts gave me an awareness of how important it was for me to establish a new and healthy identity. Although I had the understanding that I needed to change, it was a challenge to move from that knowledge to actually changing.

Role Models

My experiences with male role models left me unsatisfied. The men around me were passive. They were alcoholics and drug addicts. They were lazy and fraudulent. They were silent and emotionless. I can't think of a single man from my family who did not fit into one of those categories.

The women in my life, on the other hand, were the complete opposite. They worked and were engaged in my life, as much as they could be. They took care of me. They showed emotion.

My mother must have seen the terrible examples I was being shown by the men around me; she must have known that she alone could not correct their damaging influence. So in a move that was probably one of her best parenting moments, my mom looked to the coaches and sports directors at my school.

She noticed that these men were different than the men who were in relationship with us. They provided discipline and guidance. They had expectations, and they were incredibly reliable and involved in my life. So she did the thing that made the most sense for my future: she immersed me in sports. She saw that it was a space where I could learn some great life skills from some solid, upstanding men. And she was right. The coaches in my life did a lot to wash away the bad influence I was getting from the male role models in my immediate family.

I was lucky to have those coaches in my life and a mother who fostered those relationships. But not every kid is given this chance at redemption, and when left to their own devices, some kids do as I still did: they connect to the street. They look to other troubled kids, hoping that through them they will find their identity and family. If left without guidance, control, or support, the younger generations will end up out of control and reckless. I did.

Despite those coaches. Despite my mother. Despite knowing who my dad was.

When you lead a child toward his or her identity, a new and amazing thing can happen. The child can flourish. This is why the first step on this journey—whether or not you feel prepared or equipped or even remotely confident—is to provide the children in your life with a sense of identity.

Lead Them Toward Identity

Give your child a glimpse of a healthy role model dynamic. Dare to be the coach, the teacher, or the mentor he or she needs. Even if you are not present in the home, you can have an incredible impact by planting the seeds of identity in young men and young women. I can't promise it will always be successful—like I said, it wasn't with me—but I promise that if you don't try, it definitely won't be successful.

LESSON TWO

Transition from Untrained
to Trained

Proverbs 2:1–6 and Proverbs 3:1–6

When I committed to change, I first tried to fix myself. The harder I tried to fix myself on my own, the more frustrated I became. I was bitter and angry. I tried my own philosophies and my own tricks. Following God didn't seem like fun. It felt like a list of dos and don'ts, and I wasn't interested in that way of life. I hadn't lived under many directions or rules before, so it scared me.

For me, a man who grew up without a present father, the encouraging words found in Psalm 68:3–6 were life. I clung to them, and I knew I needed to decipher them so that I could benefit from their wisdom. As I read these words now, I can't help but think they are the words that a father would share with his child. They are words of warning, direction, correction, and loving care.

I needed to take ownership and responsibility for some things in my life. Sure, I had grown up without much of a dad. I'd had plenty of things go wrong that I could blame all my problems on. But Proverbs 2:20–21 made it clear.

One of the first things I did was apologize to my daughter's mother for how our relationship had fallen apart. It wasn't easy to admit I was wrong, but the moment I came clean, it felt as though a weight lifted off me. The hope of a romantic relationship was more than over at this point, but we still had a child to raise. It was the beginning of true change, not just for me but also for our entire situation.

As a result, my relationship with my daughter's mother improved. The drama stopped. The pettiness stopped. We became a parenting team, and for the first time, I started to see just a glimpse of what a positive co-parenting relationship dynamic looked like.

Making the Move

Most people think they can save themselves, but I found I didn't have the ability to fix myself. I tried, but it only led to more problems.

What areas of your life need to be addressed in order for you to be the parent you need to be? What past hurts do you need to forgive? What baggage do you need to let go of? In this journey toward being a better parent and role model, you will need all the help you can get, but it starts with you. It starts with your attitude. It starts when you get to the point where you don't want to recreate the cycle of destruction that you've already seen in your life. You don't want to be a fraud. You want to be the parent your kid needs you to be.

As I made this journey from untrained parent to trained parent, I followed, and continue to follow, these important truths:

1. Take responsibility for your life. This is where it started for me, and my guess is it starts here for you, too. It's time to stop blaming others for the path your life has taken. Commit to becoming the best parent you can be.

For many, taking responsibility can be the most difficult part of the process. When I decided to apologize to my daughter's mother, this did not mean she was without fault. It meant that I was going to focus on where I had dropped the ball and apologize accordingly. I did not wait for her to acknowledge her part in the deterioration. I owned my part and asked for her forgiveness. It was difficult because my pride was screaming at me to hold on to the many offenses, but I knew that there was no way I could mature if I did not take responsibility.

I also had to stop blaming my father for my poor choices. I'm reminded of the scripture Proverbs 19:3: "People ruin their lives by their own foolishness and then are angry at the LORD." Although my father's absence severely impacted me, it did not give me the right to take out my anger on other people. This cord of rage destroyed countless relationships. I felt justified in mistreating people because "my father wasn't around." That's foolishness. Until I reconciled the angry man I had become with the man I was supposed to become, my life would continue to be a mess.

Sadly, this is where many people are, but they refuse to admit it. They carry years of hurt and offenses and take it out on anyone and everyone they come in contact with. If they are parents, their children bear the brunt of their rage.

If you truly want to become a better parent, begin taking responsibility for your actions, thoughts, and attitudes today. This will more than likely require a mindset overhaul, but it will be one of the most rewarding decisions you ever make.

2. Do whatever it takes to become the best person possible. Stop waiting for someone to do it for you. Invest in personal growth. If you are interested in the Bible, study it and research it to understand what it says.

When I truly became tired of my situation, I took the steps to change it. There was no distance I wouldn't travel in order to receive the information I needed. It was time for my life to be overhauled, and it was up to me to do it.

3. Stay the course. Consistency is the key to success in anything. Your daily disciplines will make all of the difference. This is where it all comes together, and you truly begin to retrain your untrained mind to be the role model and parent you are supposed to be.

Avoid Life in "Selfie Mode"

Social media doesn't necessarily help us become better parents. For many, it forces us to live our lives in *selfie mode*, where we spend our time presenting a false picture of reality. We pretend to have it all together, which leads us to miss out on many helpful moments along the way.

As soon as I learned to ditch selfie mode and to be honest with others about my parenting struggles, I found myself surrounded by people who were willing to pour into me and positively affect my parenting. It was when I got over myself and my image that I saw the value in learning from others and their stories. Be vulnerable and allow others to come alongside you in your parenting, even if that means letting them see when you don't have it all figured out.

Put Your Child in a Good Learning Environment

As you become a trained parent, you soon learn the value of putting your child on a path of proper training and instruction. The younger you get them started, the faster they will learn the lessons that have been a lifetime coming for you.

For example, I took my oldest son, Eric, to an entrepreneurship conference so that he could meet other people and be exposed to different career tracks. This was just one way in which I helped my son understand that the sky is the limit when he applies himself.

Other things you can do include having your children learn a skill, such as computer coding, cooking, photography, or video editing. Encourage them to start their own business by raking leaves or cutting the grass for those in the community. Encourage them to volunteer and give back to the community. Push them to better themselves and increase their skills.

One of the greatest gifts we can give our children is the gift of responsibility. Many parents who had a tough upbringing attempt to shield their children from the difficulties they may have faced. While most parents don't want to see their kids suffer, there is value in a level of discomfort. When faced with challenging situations, our character and level of mental toughness are revealed. If children are too sheltered or spoiled, this could impact their ability to handle tough situations. I have learned to allow my kids the opportunity to face adversity with parental guidance so that they can gain experience and mature. I have watched them grow up a lot faster as a result of facing and overcoming adversity.

One of the biggest mistakes I have watched parents make is spoiling their children. They give them too much, causing children to develop attitudes of entitlement. It's easy for parents to fall into the trap of making life too comfortable and privileged. Oftentimes this comes from parents' own upbringings and what they might have lacked. In an effort to provide a better life, parents inadvertently handicap their kids when it comes to the real world. The result is often children who are not prepared for life's challenges because their parents did everything for them. I must admit, I myself am guilty of doing this sometimes, as I will explain in more detail later.

It could be that the parents are the ones searching for scholarships and other opportunities while the children refuse to take any responsibility for their own education. Countless parents raise their children to have the expectation that it is the parent's job to handle everything for them. I have personally witnessed parents call to ask employers to hire their teen and adult children. These parents believe they are helping, but they are stunting their children's growth, causing them to miss out on valuable life skills.

In my personal experience, I've seen that children who were spoiled struggle severely in adulthood. They were denied the opportunity to develop the skills required for success. Oftentimes these are the same adults who end up living in their parents' homes well into their thirties and forties with no clear career path or direction. Adults who struggle professionally or relationally often were allowed to develop attitudes as children and teens that centered on themselves and their likes or dislikes. This mentality does not work well in real-world scenarios and often leads to career challenges and romantic train wrecks.

This was a major issue I faced as a child as well. I was spoiled and believed that the world should revolve around me. Had I been held accountable early in life, I would have learned many of the lessons I didn't end up learning until my adult years.

Learn to Listen Actively to Your Children

Another big lesson was when I discovered I had to really sit down with my kids and listen to what was going on in their lives. It was so much easier for me to stand back and criticize and to parent from afar. But when I got involved in their lives and their thoughts, my parenting dynamic shifted in a great way.

It's not about forcing them to talk. It's about being an active listener so that when they're ready to share, you're ready to hear what they say. And I have to warn you, the hardest part of this is to avoid trying to fix the problem right away. Sometimes we all just need to feel heard and validated more than we need resolution to our struggles or frustrations. Try to be that listening ear your kids can come to, knowing that there is safety in confiding in you.

Give Teenagers Space

If your kids are teenagers and you're just now embarking on this quest to change your parenting, then you need to hear this straight from me: give them space. It's not going to be easy, but it is doable.

I've found that most teenagers who grow up with absent parents don't respond very well when those parents suddenly decide to become a part of their lives. They say, "Hey, where were you the first thirteen years? Now you want to step in and be my dad?" They're hurt. They're frustrated. They will most likely push you away.

It's not usually forever, though. Sometime in their twenties, most children begin to seek reconciliation for their damaged parental relationships. They will be less closed off, and they will make a relationship possible. While it may seem like you'll have to do a lot of waiting between now and when your child is in his or her twenties, it's worth it. But waiting doesn't mean you have to be passive.

Use these years to lay a new foundation. Attend their school events, offer to buy them lunch, and be present for holidays, birthdays, weekends, and vacations. Do all the things you failed to do early on in their lives. Even if they reject you now, as they get older, they will respond to your consistency. Eventually, they will open up to your active role as parent.

Engage in Their Lives

Engaging in their lives means putting your phone aside when you're with them. It means turning off the TV, turning down the radio, closing the computer. It means being in the moment—being completely present so that you can make the most of your time together. Remember, it is often in the mundane moments that connections are made. Be intentional with creating consistent, positive, and unique memories.

Take the time to open up and tell them your story. Share with them the emotions you felt when you were their age. Share your successes and failures. Sharing and being authentic provides opportunities for your relationship to mature. It helps them to see you as normal and human, versus being just Mom or Dad. So many parents assume a dictator role because they are fearful of being a friend. You can maintain your authority as a parent while also building a more intimate relationship with your child. Sharing your life builds credibility and creates a bond that will not be easily broken when outside influences appear. I have fun, cut up, and act silly with all of my children, but my position of Dad is not compromised. If anything, my willingness to be human with them enhances my authority as their father. I still have no problem being that strong figure they love, like, and dislike at times.

One huge mistake many parents make is to stop parenting once their child turns eighteen. The transition from teen years to adulthood can be one of the most difficult times. Your guidance is still invaluable, but keep in mind that your conversation with your young adult must reflect the life changes that are occurring. They are young adults and will appreciate it more when they are heard and talked to as adults. Don't mock their mistakes or decisions, even when they go against your advice.

Create Positive Memories

While children—especially young children—are typically happy simply spending time with their parents at home, there is nothing more powerful than creating lasting memories together by doing something special and out of the ordinary. Go for trips. Get concert tickets. Visit restaurants and parks, and attend sporting events. Do something different occasionally, even if it just means heading down the street for ice cream. Creating these positive memories could provide the leverage you need to survive those teen and young adult years.

Plan a date with each of your children individually. Choose an age-appropriate place to eat and an activity to do together—preferably something that will involve interaction. Use dates as opportunities to get to know each of your children better, make them feel loved, and create a special memory of your time together.

It Doesn't Happen Overnight

It's easy to pretend like the past doesn't matter and doesn't have a hold on us. And yet, I was living proof that the actions of a father can cause equally horrific actions in the lives of his children. Once I opened myself up to change and accepted help from others, my path took a turn.

The more you open up, the more you'll learn and the more successful you'll be at saving your family and stopping the cycle of bad parenting. As you discover and live in your identity, you will gain confidence in your parenting skills. Yes, you will make mistakes, but you will learn from them and allow those mistakes to make you a better parent.

Here is some food for thought: What type of father or mother do you want to become? When your kids are grown, what memories do you want them to carry of you and of your times together?

Many children who act out are simply crying out for the attention of a parent. Sometimes we make the mistake of using external means to try to solve issues with our children when they simply need our undivided attention and quality time.

One last note: spending time with your children also means making sure they spend time with you. This might mean cutting off their phones and computers as well as yours. The social media environment can isolate children from their parents, and vice versa. Amid the generational disconnects that many families face, social media can open a door to negative influences. While social media can also have positive aspects, it is important for parents to monitor their kids' social media activities.

Raising Fatherless Children

Over the years, I have mentored children who lacked positive paternal figures in their lives. Each child responds differently to this absence. Some adjust without major issues while others respond severely, as I did.

There are a few things I would like you to be on the lookout for, regardless of the circumstances of the absence. Most children long for the attention, affection, and love of a father. When those things are missing, kids often seek attention elsewhere. Boys and girls can have the same longing for love and attention but respond in different ways. Some may act out while others internalize their pain and turn to self-destructive behaviors.

Many parents miss these warning signs because they are still navigating their own parental issues. This is one reason why I stress having open and honest conversations about this topic. Investing in a good therapist can be beneficial. Children give us clues to what is really happening with them if we are paying attention. This requires more than dropping them off at the youth church retreat or basketball practice. It requires a focused, authentic relationship beyond such extracurricular activities.

Parental Identity

Because many parents tie their identities directly to the performance of their children, seeking help may be met with some internal resistance. If a parent is already dealing with issues, admitting these issues and seeking help for them will take intentional effort. In many cases, parents will use their children's academic or athletic successes to showcase that they are good parents. Many parents aren't able to admit shortcomings because it is a direct reflection of their own identity. In my observation, selfishness is at the core when a false image of success takes precedence over the health and well-being of the child.

Breaking the Family Cycle

Ephesians 6:4

It's one thing to work on changing yourself and your relationship with your children. It's another to work on changing a generational cycle of absent parenting in your family.

A generational cycle looks like this:

- Kids grow up with absent parents or absent-but-present parents.

- Those kids enter adulthood and have kids of their own.

- Not knowing what a healthy parenting dynamic looks like, the new parents model the absent parenting approach they experienced while growing up.

- Their kids then grow up with absent parents or absent-but-present parents, and the cycle continues.

This will go on for generations, until someone steps up and not only breaks the cycle for themselves but also helps others in their family break the cycle as well. To do this, you need to have the right tools at your disposal.

Trickle-Down Parenting

You would be amazed how much your great-great-grandparents' parenting styles influence your own—from smaller things, like not eating dinner together as a family, to larger things, such as leaving all the discipline and parenting to the women. As I stated earlier, your parenting views are largely shaped by the generations that came before you, even if those people passed away decades before you were born.

Many of our parents and grandparents never had an opportunity to experience much of a carefree childhood and were thrust into situations that forced them to grow up too quickly and without much guidance. They were often thrown into a role of caring for their younger siblings or providing financial stability for the home.

Maybe this caused their mentality to be bruised as a child. Maybe they were faced with so much responsibility early on that they shirked that responsibility later in life when it came to parenting their own children. Or maybe they just modeled what they saw around them. Whatever the case, the generations before us often grew up in tough, overwhelming situations.

My father was so damaged from his own upbringing that he was completely toxic. Once I took control and ownership of my own parenting style, I realized I needed to completely erase his influence from my life.

My mother's style was a little different. She always made sure we lived in a nice place and that I went to a good school. She kept us fed and clothed. But despite all this, she didn't know how to raise a boy—and later a man.

She didn't have a clue. My mom did everything she knew to do, but it wasn't what a son needed—it wasn't what *I* needed. A present mother and an absent father just repeated the cycle.

Again, I share my family history here because there is a code of silence in our communities. We do not talk about the past. We don't talk about damaging experiences. We figure the past is the past. It's over. Why bring it up? But it is important for us as parents to understand our own history. Unfortunately for many families, we have been trained to cover up foolishness. But if we fail to understand our history and reconcile it with what we need to change, we will perpetuate the problems. We will rehash the same broken parenting styles that didn't work for our grandparents, parents, or us.

A major turning point in my life was when I became committed to understanding my family history. Why was there so much dysfunction? Where did my mother learn her parenting skills? What kind of parenting did my grandparents experience?

As I peeled back the layers, I discovered my maternal grandfather was fatherless. My grandmother was also raised in dysfunction—and this was just on my mother's side. My father's side had more dysfunction, more sad stories, and more absent fathers and family lies.

Trickle-down parenting is responsible for so much more than our own parenting habits. It's also responsible for our physical and mental health challenges, as well as our work ethic. For many, it's responsible for how we view God and faith. We then pass these things down to our own children, who pass them on to their children, in turn. At what point do we take a step back and ask ourselves if we're getting it right? At what point do we identify the unhealthy mindsets, practices, and habits that follow our families from generation to generation and become part of our legacies?

Taking Out Our Hidden Issues on Our Kids

Sometimes one of the most difficult lessons to learn is that we're wrong. Whether it is pride and arrogance, or just stupidity, there are times when we think we're doing a good job at something, but we're really not. One of the most common ways we fail without knowing it is in our hidden issues.

Over the years, I have observed many parents who unknowingly pass down their hidden (and not-so-hidden) issues to their children. Whether it is passing down their insecurities, anger, materialism, poor lifestyle habits, faulty belief systems, or simply bad communication habits, I often see the bad influences of previous generations flowing down to the children. These parents love their children but do not understand how they let their own backgrounds impact their parenting.

For example, if parents were raised eating fast food on a nightly basis, it is no surprise to see them passing this same unhealthy habit to their children. If parents were never taught how to manage their financial resources properly, there is a good chance their children will never be taught how to manage their finances. If parents were placed in front of the television for unlimited hours per day, there is a good chance this will be their parenting style as well. The list goes on and on.

I had to be intentional about discovering these bad habits of my own, unpacking them, and making the uncomfortable but necessary changes. Remember, some of these issues may be hidden, and we may have to dig deep to find them. My encouragement is to surround yourself with other healthy parents if possible. If your situation does not allow for a healthy parenting community, I encourage you to take advantage of the wealth of free knowledge offered on platforms like YouTube. In some cases, professional counseling is a good option to address these issues. Whatever your situation, I encourage you to take action today.

Your Life—Your Story

You have your own unique story to reflect upon. Here are a few questions I want you to ponder. Take some time to examine these questions, because they relate to key areas in changing the generational narrative for your family. They may be uncomfortable, but they are necessary for healing to occur.

1. What habits, traits, or behaviors have been passed down to you that you do not want your children to have passed down to them?

2. What habits, traits, or behaviors have already been passed down to your children that need to change? This may require having some honest introspection and conversations to get to the root of the challenges.

Focusing on these two questions will help you establish a new foundation. Perhaps you have been verbally aggressive and harsh toward your children. Perhaps you have been physically abusive toward them. Perhaps you have placed your own career or romantic relationships ahead of them. Perhaps you enabled and spoiled your children. Perhaps you overprotected them and did not prepare them for the real world. Whatever the case, take a moment to reflect and be brutally honest. Today is the day things can begin to change.

Oftentimes all a parent needs to do is show humility and apologize. Sometimes that is enough to open the door for the child to be free. So many parents choose to become defensive about their parenting mistakes, which makes healing any wounds difficult. If we are willing to admit our mistakes, we can establish a parenting foundation for the generations to come and become game changers for our children's children's children.

Crisis with Our Children

Part of my mission as an adult has been to help children and youth avoid making costly mistakes. I have spent more than twenty years teaching and leading youth. I can see myself in many of the boys and girls I have led and mentored over the years, which gives me a unique ability to connect with them. I can recall the need for a strong but compassionate male figure as early as four years of age. I can recall needing to hear a man encourage me when I was angry or discipline me when I was in need of it.

Over the years, as a director of a summer program for youth, several scenarios in particular have impacted me. There was a ten-year-old girl who was caught sharing pornography on her smartphone. When we sat down to speak with her, she stated that she learned it from her mother. When the matter was brought to the attention of her mother, her mother opted to remove her from the program due to her own embarrassment. While her embarrassment was understandable, her daughter had just begun to thrive in the program, yet her mom caused her to leave the very thing that was beginning to help her.

I also remember a six-year-old boy who told me that he wanted to commit suicide when he became angry. When we attempted to inform his parents, they did not respond to any of our attempts to reach them. They appeared to be a very religious family, and I was left in dismay at their avoidance of their son's issue.

My experiences have shown me the depth of pain, neglect, negative influences, and insecurities our children are facing. Many parents are clueless or couldn't care less.

The amount of exposure to negative influences that our elementary students and middle-schoolers encounter is staggering. And sad. Much of the exposure comes from how the parents choose to raise their children.

Honest Conversations

If we want to change the culture, we need to have honest conversations. If we want to have maximum impact, we need to get real with one another. We need to share the things that we'd rather forget. Sometimes relatives do not want to have these kinds of conversations. They don't want to know the truth. They prefer to stay ignorant. They prefer to assume that everything is fine and that while there may be bumps along the way, we all make it out okay in the end.

But we're not all making it out okay. We're not all fine in the end.

If the first step to eliminating dysfunction is to break the code of silence, then it's time to do so. Ask the tough questions. Speak out when bad behavior is being exemplified by dear family members. It's tough to do, but it's necessary.

But calling out or talking about dysfunction isn't enough. We need to go further. What else is needed to foster healthy family environments in which all members are actively contributing to help stop the cycles of dysfunction and protect future generations?

An Honest Conversation with My Daughter

Part of breaking the cycles of dysfunction is having tough conversations. I was faced with this when my daughter was fourteen years old. It was one of the most difficult conversations I've ever had, but I knew it was necessary and that it needed to happen at that time.

My daughter is from a previous relationship prior to my marriage. I was twenty-one years old when she was born. I was so excited to be a father that I never considered she might not be my biological child. As the years passed, however, I wasn't one hundred percent sure she was mine biologically. Part of me was content as things were, but another part of me wanted to know the truth, either way.

This happens with a lot of families. There are paternity question marks on one or more children, and the doubts become the elephant in the room. The doubts and questions cause strife and lead to even more identity issues, which take a tremendous toll on children once they discover the truth. These issues lead to the same cycles we may spend a lifetime trying to break. With this in mind, I realized I needed to know for certain if she was my biological daughter.

I took the first of two paternity tests when my daughter was nine years old. Waiting for the results was very tense, and the "what ifs" constantly went through my mind until the results came back. On a chilly day in 2002, the results arrived. I looked at the envelope knowing that once I opened it, there was no turning back. I could leave it sealed and continue life as before, or I could open it and know the truth.

What I also knew was that whatever was in the envelope was part of the larger plan, and there was a blessing in store. So with great anxiety, I opened the envelope, and the results forever changed my family's life. The results revealed that my daughter, the little girl who had changed my life and whom I had spent nine years raising, was not my biological daughter. My heart was crushed, but I immediately began to look at it from a different perspective. To be clear, my daughter's mother and I were not in a relationship when I thought she was conceived. I was living a reckless life, and our encounter was a one-time occurrence. Unbeknownst to both of us, she was already pregnant.

God knew the truth from the very beginning. For whatever reason, I never thought to have the test done when my daughter was a baby. But God used this child to change my life. It went so much deeper than biology. God sent my daughter to save my life, and there was no way I was going to throw her away to fend for herself because of my new discovery. I realized that despite all of the mess I had been in at twenty-one years old, God allowed this child to be placed into my care. I had committed to care for her before she was born, and that was not going to change.

This was one of the most profound moments of my life. The grief of losing my biological daughter was quickly replaced with the joy of knowing that God had entrusted me with this little girl at the perfect time in my life. It was surreal, but not without challenges. How would my wife respond? How would my daughter respond?

The day I discovered that my daughter and I were not biologically related was the same day her mother faced a major medical problem that required her to be hospitalized for an extended period of time. I decided that this was not the best time to reveal the paternity matter to my daughter. Additionally, I was aware that she was only nine years old. How would she process all of this information? What would the long-term implications be for her? I had joint legal custody and had legal protections in place, but the situation was tough.

Her mother's recovery took several years. Over those years, certain people close to me said that I should keep the paternity information to myself and act as if everything were normal. I knew that would require me to live a lie, though. It would also require me to take a choice away from my daughter and possibly prevent another man from ever knowing about his biological daughter. There were so many dynamics, but she needed to know the truth so that she could make decisions for herself. I also needed to fill her in on the discovery before she became an adult. This was a true parenting moment in the making.

I decided to have one more paternity test to confirm, and the same results came back. At this point, my daughter was fourteen. We needed to have an honest conversation, and I had to prepare myself. She could get angry. She might even reject me. Telling her the truth was one of the most difficult things I have ever done, but I don't regret it for a moment. It was the truth, and it allowed her to choose to pursue her biological father if she wished.

When I told her about her true paternity, she was very emotional but said plainly that nothing was going to change—that I was her *Daddy*. In that moment, I saw God at work and His transformation in me manifesting in this little girl. I told her that God had sent her into my life to save me and had changed me to make sure she didn't repeat the same cycle.

Surround Yourself with the Right People

When my daughter was born and I became committed to making changes and doing right by her—even though I knew little about what "doing right" meant—one of the best decisions I made was to focus on my emotional and spiritual health. I knew I needed to be around people who were doing something positive with their lives, and for other people's lives, too.

As a family, surround yourselves with the people who will provide support for you as parents and grandparents. Find people who will encourage you and teach you things you may not know—people who will let you model after them. In other words, find people who are living the family life you want to live, and seek their support and guidance.

Listen to Your Child's Heart

So many children carry secrets because their parents don't listen to them when they speak. I recall having a conversation with a young lady who stated that she was molested by her cousin from the time she was in kindergarten until she was in second grade. When she came forward with the allegations at age eleven, her father dismissed her claims and became verbally abusive toward her mother. He accused both of them of lying and led a campaign to discredit his daughter's claims. I could hear her pain when speaking with her. Her own father had already abandoned her by his absence in her life as a child, and now he was rejecting her. My advice to her was to:

1. Stand on the truth. Truth is true no matter what others say.

2. Do not allow anger to turn into bitterness. Bitterness is a poison that only destroys.

3. Maintain and establish healthy boundaries should anyone become verbally abusive, including parents.

4. Understand that abuse is very common in families and communities. Victims of abuse should know they aren't alone.

5. Know that evil can be turned to good by sharing your story to help others.

6. Develop compassion for others who experience the same type of trauma.

7. Never allow someone to steal your smile and innocence.

8. Stay focused on commitments and responsibilities and on doing your best. Pain is

never an excuse.

9. Allow God to heal you.

10. Seek professional counseling to help navigate the difficulties of the situation. We were designed to encourage each other, and that includes being encouraged.

At the conclusion of the conversation, she was very appreciative. Possibly this was a pivotal moment in her life. She was able to be heard and encouraged to remain truthful and positive. I could not help but think: What would have happened if she had never had that conversation with me? How would the alleged abuse from her cousin and rejection from her father have begun to manifest in her life? Unfortunately, many children, teens, and adults have no one to talk to about what they face. As a result, they take out their pain and frustrations on the easiest target: their own children. And so the cycle continues.

Is Your Child Prey for Predators?

I have encountered many young women and men who have been victims of sexual abuse at the hands of authority figures who were supposed to protect them. I have often wondered how this is able to occur undetected for so long. The reality is that there are cultures of abuse within some of our schools, families, and religious institutions that are able to function because of silence and cover-up. We see news reports regularly of a teacher or religious leader crossing the line with a child. Many of these children live in two-parent homes, but the parents are clueless until it comes out. How does this occur? There are many variables that contribute to adults preying on our children and youth. I believe the best way to combat it is by educating our parents and children about the behavior and tactics of predators.

Children who have certain emotional deficiencies may be more susceptible to being lured into these very damaging adult/child relationships. My advice is that you are mindful of who you allow your child to spend alone time with. Single parents, be mindful of the alone time you allow your child to spend with your boyfriend or girlfriend. While we want to assume the best, there are countless accounts of abuses occurring in these scenarios. There are many boyfriends or girlfriends who would never violate a child, but keeping your antennae up and staying alert can ensure healthy interactions with your child.

Monitoring your children's phones and social media accounts can reveal a great deal about their relationships. Long-term effects of relationships may not manifest until many years later. As parents, it is our job to protect our children to the best of our abilities. Stay vigilant!

Get Help!

Seeking professional therapy or counseling can be one of the best investments you make. Counseling is frowned upon in some communities. Sadly, many of these communities are also plagued with numerous problems: drug and alcohol abuse, teen suicides, and other disorders. I cannot help but think these issues are related. These problems manifest because we are carrying so much dead weight in our hearts. When we get past the negative stigma of mental therapy, our families can begin to heal. And healing starts with us as parents.

When flying on an airplane, we are reminded to put our oxygen masks on first and then help others. The same principle applies in life. If we take care of ourselves, we will be in a much better position to help others. Unfortunately, many families prioritize entertainment, outer appearances, or spending money on depreciating items rather than investing in the mental and spiritual health of themselves and their families. If you want to break the cycle in your family, I encourage you to seek advice from wise counselors who have the best interests of you and your family at heart.

There is value in the advice of others. Proverbs 15:22 says, "Plans go wrong for lack of advice; many advisers bring success."

Put Away Your Toys

When I was a child, I spoke and thought and reasoned as a child. But when I grew up, I put away childish things.
—1 Corinthians 13:11

As I was becoming a man and a father, I knew there were some things I needed to put away. I knew I needed to stop getting drunk, stop chasing women, and stop smoking weed—especially since it was illegal at the time. These were the obvious indulgences in my life that I needed to get rid of, but there were less obvious ones, too: I needed to stop being selfish, always putting myself before others. I needed to stop trying to control my own life.

Just as I needed to get rid of the childish things in my life and become the father I needed to be, you and your family need to make a similar transition if you're going to end the cycle of bad parenting.

It's time to stop overeating, let go of self-seeking tendencies, and drop all unhealthy, promiscuous behavior. It's time to clean up the words that come out of your mouth, as Ephesians 4:29 tells us. It's time to get serious about holding a steady job and doing what needs to be done to provide food, shelter, and clothing (2 Thessalonians 3:7–12).

It's time to grow up.

Freedom

Successful parenting requires self-examination. This is also true if you're an aunt or uncle, or a grandmother or grandfather. You have the power of influence over the children in your life. Examine your heart. Seek out the generational dysfunction that has been plaguing you for decades and dare to make some of these changes together.

I didn't want my daughter to see her father as a promiscuous drunk. I didn't want her to see the worst side of me. I didn't want her to think that was how a man was supposed to act. I didn't want her to repeat the cycle and marry someone just like me. So I made a change.

I dug into my family's history. I went to the core of how we had gotten to where we were as a family. Now my daughter can look at me and see a healthy example of a man. She can see us trying to break the cycle, to create a clean slate for her and her future. She can see when we fall short, but she can also see how we persevere.

Today, I have four children—one girl and three boys. Every day, I am thankful for the transformation that occurred in my life because of my daughter. It has allowed me to give the same care and attention to all three of my sons. But it breaks my heart when I turn on the TV and see the terrible cycles perpetuated in our communities—stories of dysfunction, generation after generation. And very little is changing.

Let's dare to look upon our history. Let's set a new standard from this day forward, and let's work together to walk in a new direction. Grandparents, parents, children, aunts, uncles, let's do this for the young ones before us today and the ones who are yet to be born. If there is a cycle to be broken, I want you to dare to do it. No matter your ethnicity, no matter where you come from, no matter your income, there is dysfunction in every family. This is for all people from all communities.

Take this wisdom. Apply it to your story.

If appropriate and possible, it may be beneficial to interview older members of your extended family to find out about the type of homes in which your parents and grandparents grew up. Looking back beyond your own parents and childhood, what is your family's parenting history? If you are married, what is your spouse's family history? Are there any good parenting traits that you want to hold on to and pass down?

LESSON FOUR

The Importance of Wisdom

Proverbs 4:1–9

In Proverbs 4, we find a father pleading with his children to follow his advice, avoid evil, and seek after wisdom. Throughout this passage, he shares both the dangers of veering from the path of wisdom and the reward for staying the course. In essence, this is a love letter from a father to his children. He is offering his very best advice and help, holding nothing back, and giving his children all he has so that they may live positive, fruitful lives.

In today's culture, we often feel like we are giving our children all that we have, yet we often grumble and complain about it. We tend to view our children as a burden. We've been programmed to focus on the hardships of parenting, the sacrifice it takes, the things we have to give up, and the money we have to spend. This is a dangerous mentality, and our children pick up on it. They can tell the difference between parents who happily and gratefully sacrifice for their children and those who do so with disdain.

Sacrificial parents exercise wisdom, while those who parent with disdain are fools.

Wisdom in Parenting

There is no greater form of accountability than being responsible for the development of another person's life. It is one of the highest callings. The kind of people our children become is a direct result of our parenting presence, or lack thereof, in our children's lives. This is why having and seeking wisdom is so important. Through wisdom, we can know the proper way to bring a child up, even if we never had this exemplified for us.

> But the way of the wicked is like total darkness. They have no idea what they are stumbling over.
> —Proverbs 4:19

The alternative to wisdom is to learn the hard way. Verse 19 talks about the way of the wicked being dark; these wandering people don't know what they're stumbling over. They're trying to move forward, but they're struggling.

This was me. I lacked wisdom, and my life was like the blind leading the blind. I did what others were doing. I listened to bad advice, and in the process, I was far from where I was supposed to be.

But once I realized my incredible need for wisdom, my life changed. I realized my parenting strategies were all wrong; my life strategies were all wrong. And it was time to make them right.

Wisdom in Discipline

If kids feel they are unloved, they become angry, frustrated, and confused, which leads to them acting out and disobeying. It sets a tone for their entire life: that they don't need to listen to anyone. They feel that since the adults in their lives don't really care about them, then they shouldn't care about those adults.

Providing a loving, nurturing environment for your children is key to avoiding many of the behavioral issues that parents face. A supportive home—with loving parents who help their children grow and become responsible, mature adults—is the foundation that a child needs.

When there is a need to discipline children, it should come from parents' desires to lovingly correct their children and instill wisdom, rather than from anger or frustration.

Growing up, the families in my neighborhood had a very different take on discipline. Kids were often beaten or abused with an extension cord, all in the name of discipline. Then we grew up, thinking that was an acceptable way to handle misbehavior, so we did the same to our own kids. This example is one of the worst parts of trickle-down parenting. We repeat violent cycles just as easily as we repeat absent parenting or negativity. Then we wonder why our children grow up and act out. We wonder why they don't listen. As parents, it's our duty to use wisdom to discipline and train our children lovingly.

Wisdom in discipline means only disciplining out of love, never out of anger. Listen to your child. Seek to understand the behavior. What was the logic? Can you have a conversation to correct or influence that thinking? Consider what a natural consequence may be—which isn't extreme, excessive, or abusive—that will help the child truly learn from the experience.

Wisdom in Family Relations

Another area in which we parents sometimes lack wisdom is that of complex family situations. The modern American family can take on many different shapes, such as blended families, divorced families, and adoptive families. It's important to exercise wisdom when dealing with these sensitive dynamics.

Wisdom says that if you are a single parent, you should be careful about whom you date and how often you change dating partners. Be careful whom you introduce to your children. The last thing your kids need is for dad to have a new girlfriend enter the home every few months.

Wisdom also says you should consider a new boyfriend or girlfriend's story. Is this someone who has confronted his or her own trickle-down parenting issues, or is it someone who will bring unresolved baggage? Remember, this person will impact your children the moment they meet. If you choose to marry someone with kids, then remember that you are marrying the entire family, and he or she is marrying yours. For your family to be strong and stable, it can't be *your kids* and *my kids*. It has to be *our kids*.

Wisdom in Honesty

The biggest bit of wisdom we can give to our kids, especially when they cross over into adulthood, is honesty. Be honest about your own mistakes. Be clear about what you've learned and how you grew. Help them understand that your greatest goal in life is for them to be better humans and better parents than you are.

Do this by being fully engaged. Be realistic with yourself about your child's strengths and weaknesses. Be committed and involved, but don't lose yourself in your children, either. Continue to be a loving husband or wife and a committed member of the community.

The Wisdom in Wisdom

If you're looking for one big takeaway from this book,

this is it: seek wisdom. Live your life as an example of wisdom. By planting these seeds now, you will reap a harvest of reward when they become teenagers and cross over into adulthood.

Do you view your children as a burden or a blessing? How is your view demonstrated in your attitude and actions toward them? What needs to change in your attitude and actions so that your children sense that you truly view them as a blessing?

Contrast disciplining in love and disciplining in anger. What should you do when your own anger threatens to become out of control? What are the pitfalls of being too passive and not disciplining at all? What are some creative and effective means for needed correction?

Plan some focused time with your child or children this week. Tell them a story from your life about a lesson you learned the hard way. Consider their age when choosing what story to relate to them. Encourage them to learn from your mistake—and from your wisdom.

LESSON FIVE

Make the Most of Your Time

Proverbs 5:1–8

I've heard it said that the days of parenthood are long, but the years are short. This is absolutely true. The daily grind can be tough. Those days spent with young children can be draining. We wonder if it will ever end. Will these babies ever grow to be teenagers? Will these teenagers ever be out on their own?

Then we blink and it's over. The years fly by, though the days sometimes drag. Consequently, in the chaos of the daily grind of parenting, it may seem like we have all the time in the world to turn the ship around and right our wrongs. "Tomorrow, I'll practice good discipline." "Tomorrow, I'll have that talk with my kid about respect." "Tomorrow, I'll plan that fun outing." But in reality, we have only a brief blip of time, a small window in which to make our impact. Every moment that we spend being distracted, every interaction that results in anger or selfishness, is a moment we will never get back.

We've only been given so much time. And as I've said before, change does not happen overnight. A seed planted today does not reap a harvest tomorrow. It takes time, dedication, and perseverance. If you want change, you have to begin now!

Time for Change

Time is not only something that you will have to deal with when it comes to leading your children down a better path. You'll also have to deal with the time it takes for those around you to accept your new way of life.

Making the choice to stop getting drunk or high, and to put your kids first, may not sit well with many of your friends. They'll want the old you back, the guy who stayed out late and was up for anything.

Others, especially family members, may question your new lifestyle. They may be fearful that it will turn you into someone they don't recognize—someone who makes them feel guilty or "less than."

In many cases, it will take time for those around you to see that your life change is the best thing that has ever happened to you. In the meantime, if they mock the new you, then you may need to take the difficult step of either removing those people from your life or downgrading their role in it.

If you find that your circle of friends does not ultimately support your new life, then it may be time to find new friends.

Time for Improvement

Imagine you are sailing in the ocean on a thousand-mile journey. Simply adjusting your course by even a few degrees will completely change the trajectory of where you will land! Even though a full life-change takes time, you will start seeing small results immediately. Gradually, those small adjustments will lead to big transformation. You may be months or years from making landfall, yet you'll soon begin noticing the small changes that will eventually add up to significant differences in your life and relationships.

One of the best ways to help the process of planting positive seeds is to gain control over the tongue:

> *The tongue can bring death or life; those who love to talk will reap the consequences.*
> **—Proverbs 18:21**

Negative statements shape our kids. Profanity shapes our kids. Song lyrics shape our kids. Every word that we say or that is said to our children has an impact on them.

I will never forget the time I was on a flight from Orlando to Baltimore/Washington. A mother was hurling the most profane words at her children as if it were normal, daily conversation. Initially, I was offended, but then I thought about what her childhood must have been like. Perhaps this was learned behavior that she was passing down to her children. I could only imagine the impact her words were having on her sons and future generations.

What words are we allowing into our children's ears? What television shows are we letting them watch? What video games are they playing? When we interact with them, how do we treat them? Do we show respect, or do we exercise our dominance? Do we engage them in conversation, or do we tell them what to do?

Over time, all words have an impact. Words can build up, and words can tear down. Every day, we have the opportunity to plant seeds of positivity through our words and through the words that we allow to enter our child's world. And remember, seeds sprout. So, whatever you are sowing will one day manifest its own harvest—for better or worse. Be extra-intentional about what seeds you are planting, because they will sprout one day.

Beyond Words

Just as we must get our words under control, we also need to consider our actions. You may need to break a smoking habit. You may need to start eating healthier or going to the gym. You may need to get some negative music out of your life. You may need to clean up what you're watching on TV. You may need to start to read more and take in healthy influences.

The list of things we can do to become better examples for our children is endless, and that's why we must start today. Time is fleeting. When we put things off for tomorrow, we are actively choosing not to make a difference today.

Pain in the Process

Change is a process, which requires time, and a day delayed is a day lost. You may need to say goodbye to some things that you enjoy doing and begin saying hello to some new habits. Clean up your words and mind your actions, because your children are watching and every negative statement or destructive action prevents your seeds from growing. Don't let your words and actions delay the harvest.

How do the people in your life respond to the changes you are making? Are they supportive or dismissive? Whose influences do you need to limit or remove from your life?

Describe the words that your children hear from you. Are your words building up or tearing down? Do you react in anger or direct your children in love? Do you complain and grow exasperated often? Are your children hearing profanity, sensual talk, or violent threats from anyone in your home or any media influences?

Reflect on a time when you planned to do something

with or for your child yet never got around to it—at least, not until after he or she had outgrown the opportunity or it was no longer available. What are some essential things to instill in your children right now, while you still have time?

For one week, keep track of how much focused time you spend with your child or children. This could be time eating together, playing together, doing homework, or even riding in the car together, as long as there is interaction. Where are you doing a good job being focused and intentional, and where are you unnecessarily distracted? How can you incorporate your children into the routine of life in a more intentional way (e.g., letting them help make dinner, work in the yard together, care for a pet, etc.)?

LESSON SIX

Exercising Common Sense

Proverbs 8:12–21

So often we think that to be a good parent, we should be able to give our kids whatever they want: toys, games, electronics. We save up for a private school education. We think, *"If only I could enroll them in that expensive sports activity, I'll be a good parent."* In today's culture, we chase money rather than wisdom. We put all our hopes in college education but forget about common sense.

But Proverbs 8 is clear: money, status, wealth, and material things do not make us good parents or good humans. Nothing is more valuable than knowledge, discernment, and common sense.

Children are a gift from the LORD; they are a reward from him.
—Psalm 127:3

This seems like common sense. *Of course* children are a gift. Of course they are a blessing. Yet we let so much time pass by without fully taking that to heart and believing it. We lack the common sense needed to see the incredible blessing that is before us.

How many other areas of our lives lack common sense? In how many other areas are we failing to see the problems staring us right in the face? And how much more effective would we be as parents if we were to open our eyes and use common sense to address the realities of parenting in today's culture?

Common sense is in short supply nowadays because what was once commonly agreed on as wisdom and good sense is now controversial. It's no coincidence that as our culture has redefined what is good, common sense has become increasingly rare. That is why we must be intentional about fostering it in our families.

Common Sense About Money Matters for Parents

While chasing money and material things can serve as a major distraction for many parents, financial instability can be equally distracting. Poor financial management is never a good thing and can affect our children in many ways. Just as negative emotional behaviors can be passed from generation to generation, negative financial habits can be passed down, too. These habits will most likely affect their health, marriages, careers, and children. I spent many years making bad financial decisions because I was financially uneducated. My mother did not have good financial habits, and my father was absent. I had to be intentional about changing my financial future.

Money is seen in a negative light in many religious circles, but there are countless scriptures that emphasize the importance of properly managing our resources:

> *Take a lesson from the ants, you lazybones. Learn from their ways and become wise! Though they have no prince or governor or ruler to make them work, they labor hard all summer, gathering food for the winter. But you, lazybones, how long will you sleep? When will you wake up? A little extra sleep, a little more slumber, a little folding of the hands to rest—then poverty will pounce on you like a bandit; scarcity will attack you like an armed robber.*
>
> **—Proverbs 6:6–11**

> *Just as the rich rule the poor, so the borrower is servant to the lender.*
>
> **—Proverbs 22:7**

> *Lazy people want much but get little, but those who work hard will prosper.*
>
> **—Proverbs 13:4**

I decided I would not pass a negative financial legacy down to my children. My focus was to become financially literate and to establish a new standard. This conviction did not come from a materialistic mindset; rather, it came from wanting my children to establish a strong financial foundation and not simply get by paying the bills each month.

The first step was recognizing how culture influenced my financial decisions. The majority of the people I knew suffered from poor money management habits and always seemed to be lacking financially in some respect. I do not recall talking about money management at any point in my childhood. As a result, I suffered financially in adulthood. I cannot emphasize enough the importance of good money management skills. Reducing your expenses, maintaining a good income level, and protecting your assets are basic practices that can keep you in a good financial position.

One mistake many parents make is overworking at the expense of their children. The rationale is that work provides a better life for our families, but parents often fail to see that overworking results in neglect of our families and children. Oftentimes this neglect leaves children vulnerable to all kinds of negative influences. I strongly encourage parents to map a healthy financial plan before embarking upon additional work, only taking on extra if necessary.

Financial stability can help a family on many levels. Unfortunately, I have seen many families without solid financial plans. They are vulnerable on multiple levels, from a lack of life insurance, disability insurance, and long-term care insurance for themselves and their children to a lack of savings and no estate plan. If you truly want to be a game changer, become financially educated.

Common Sense for a Young Generation

Children today live through their smartphones and games. They are constantly connected to the world around them through electronic devices and social media platforms. It's common to feel as though you need to compete for their attention. It's sometimes natural to want to jump to an extreme and take away all of their games and devices.

But common sense says there should be a balance. Our children need to learn how to live in a world of technology, but they also need to learn how to break away from the lure of technology. They need to learn responsibility and how to engage with others on a personal level even when it might be easier to shoot off a text. They need healthy control over their devices.

One way to combat this is by traveling. That's right: take a trip. As a child, my family did not place a priority on traveling. As a result, my worldview was limited and skewed. Technology, especially smartphones, only fosters this. Traveling opens up their world. Now that I'm a father, I encourage my children to travel so that they can learn first-hand about other people, circumstances, and viewpoints. I give them space to establish their own perspectives—with guidance, of course!

I encourage parents to find ways to distance their children from their electronic devices every once in a while. Introduce them to the beauty of the world around them and the importance of real-life relationships. It's all about balance. This kind of parenting can't be bought. It's right in front of you, and it just takes a bit of common sense to determine what is best for your child.

Parenting Doesn't Stop at Age Eighteen

Recognizing the transition points in your relationship with your children is one of the most important aspects of parenting. Your children will grow up. Detecting when the conversations need to mature is important. Many parents miss these transition points and hinder their children's maturation process.

One of the most difficult transition points is from adolescence to adulthood. Many parents remove their hands too soon, while other parents hold on too long. Our children need us as parents for a lifetime, but the relationships must evolve over the years. Recognizing these points will pay dividends for generations.

One of my sons began a new relationship when he was seventeen, with all of the teen hormones and emotions that come with that territory. I instantly remembered when I was faced with the same feelings as a teen and had no one to guide me through the process. As a father, I knew my role was to help him think through what he was feeling and to encourage him to make wise decisions. When he was eleven, I could make the decisions for him. But seventeen-year-olds should be allowed the space to make certain decisions for themselves, while still being guided through the process. I try to remain mindful of transition points such as this and not miss opportunities by being preoccupied or overbearing. To be clear, there will still be circumstances in which I need to jump in and be more involved, but my goal is to raise men, not over-sheltered little boys.

At some point, my sons may become fathers, and my prayer is that I will have planted positive seeds that benefit my grandchildren and break the cycle of dysfunction that was passed down to me. Recognize when your children are growing up, and adjust relationships accordingly.

Learning from Past Parenting Mistakes

What do you do when you screw things up? Making mistakes is a part of parenting. When I look back at what I would have done differently, overcompensating is the number one thing that comes to mind. I did too much and did not allow my children to experience enough of the challenges of real life. They were sheltered, spoiled, and protected from many things that would have helped them mature. This developed a mentality of entitlement and, on many levels, laziness.

The question I have asked myself is: "Why did I overcompensate for my children?" Number one, I was never properly trained to be father. Number two, I wanted them to know I supported them one hundred percent and did not want them to feel the rejection I had felt as a child. Number three, I did not want them to be exposed to the toxic situations in which I had involved myself.

My intentions were well-placed, but I went too far. Does this mean I was a failure as a parent? By no means, because I was able to recognize and adjust my parenting style to reflect my new understanding.

When my oldest son was awarded a full scholarship to college, then lost it because he didn't apply himself to the curriculum—and then lied about his situation—I adjusted. Instead of offering to pay for college, I gave him a deadline to start paying rent to live in my home. There was no legitimate excuse for lying about losing the scholarship, and he needed to feel the impact of his decisions. Dad and Mom would not bail him out of the situation he had created.

When my middle son started to act in similar ways to me at his age, I imposed the consequences I should have received. I wished someone had stepped up for me and given me some boundaries so that perhaps I could have avoided some trouble. So as parents, my wife and I held our son accountable. It was difficult because he was spoiled and not used to the severity of the consequences we levied upon him, but we did it anyway. Being a parent means doing what your kids need, even if it isn't what they want.

Diet Mistakes

In all of my efforts to break generational bad habits, there was one I passed down, not fully aware of its impact: poor diet. I was not aware of the impact of an unhealthy diet until I was well into my thirties and was facing some health realities of my own.

My foundation for poor dietary choices was established in my childhood, and unfortunately, I passed it down to my children. When my kids were younger, we ate at fast food restaurants on a weekly basis. We cooked at home most of the time, but even meals we deemed as healthy were loaded with sugar and salt. Their palates became accustomed to eating high-salt, high-sugar diets because that is what they grew up eating. Trying to change their diets now has been a monumental challenge. My focus is to educate them and, more importantly, to model the change in my own habits.

Today, I understand how important a healthy diet is. I am a witness to how poor eating habits manifest into all kinds of chronic illnesses and obesity. Teens often don't understand the implications of a poor diet, as their fast metabolisms and more active lifestyles burn a high number of calories.

One of our sons had eleven cavities as an eighteen-year-old as a result of his sugar addiction. Although he made the decision to consume endless amounts of sugar after we had warned him about the potential effects, we were responsible for introducing a high-sugar diet into his life while he was a young child.

I encourage you to begin the process of gradually establishing a healthy food culture in your home, which will become another part of the legacy you leave behind. Although I passed down poor dietary choices during my kids' earlier years, my wife and I have been aggressively trying to change the dynamic. I hope that my children will establish a healthy food lifestyle for themselves.

Establishing a household culture of good physical health will pay dividends for generations to come. No matter how much education we have or how much money we make, good health is priceless.

Common Sense for Young Parents

Being a young parent can be difficult. Juggling life and parenting can seem like an insurmountable task. But it's not an excuse. You can't simply put your parenting years on hold because you're too busy getting your degree or trying to establish a career. While money and success may seem like the ticket to a better life, nothing will help you as much as investing in yourself and your family. Join a support group. Take that class on personal growth. Learn about responsible living, personal finance, and more. Do whatever it takes to make wisdom your goal as you carefully put your children above your desire for a better job, a better paycheck, or a personal vacation.

Common Sense for Distance Parenting

If you're in the difficult situation of being an incarcerated parent—or if you're stepping in and helping to parent children whose biological parents are incarcerated—then the best thing you can do is help maintain the relationship between parent and child.

Encourage letters, phone calls, and visits as often as possible. Have patience as you work with the children and encourage them to open up to you. Be honest and up front about mistakes made and let the children know they do not have to repeat the same mistakes. At the same time, make it clear that their parents love them and that they have not been abandoned. Celebrate every accomplishment—and remember birthdays!

These efforts let children know they are loved and valued. If we want to break the school-to-prison pipeline, let's use every tool available to maintain and encourage a positive connection between parent and child when incarceration is involved.

The same can be said for distance parenting in general. Sometimes when parents separate, one parent moves out of state or even out of the country. If you are the distant parent, be there for your children. Make the extra effort not just to be there "when possible." Those words usually turn into "never." Rather, make an effort to be there even when it's difficult and inconvenient. Take the time to make it clear that your children are loved and have not been abandoned. Again, don't forget birthdays!

If you are the parent who is primarily raising your children, don't talk negatively about the distant parent. Resist the temptation to be snide about her mother. Fight the urge to degrade his father. As I said, my mother never once spoke negatively about my father. Follow her example.

Common Sense for Overworked Parents

There will be times when work will suck a lot of your time and energy. There will be times when it's all you can do to put food on the table and a roof over your family's head. Though these times in life are difficult, they are more common than you think. So many parents face these kinds of challenges. However, you are not alone. It's important to know that being busy at work is not a good enough excuse to put your parenting on hold.

Resist the temptation to neglect your kids. Put a strategy in place with people you trust who can step in when your season of life gets particularly busy. Seek help from others. And know that this busy time will not last forever. If you are investing in yourself and pushing forward, you will have victory over this difficult season of life.

The Basics of Common Sense

At the end of the day, common sense comes down to asking this question: What decision will improve my parenting and my relationship with my kids?

Anytime you are faced with a problem or a setback, ask that question. The answer you come up with should be one of wisdom, knowledge, and common sense. It's going to be the right decision for your family, and you can confidently move forward.

What are some things—material items or

opportunities—that you have equated with being a good parent? How does each miss the mark? What can you replace those things with, to truly implement good parenting?

Considering your children's ages and your family dynamics, what is a healthy balance for their technology usage? How much television and computer/ phone/ device screen time should they typically have? How will you monitor this and keep them accountable, as well as protect them from dangerous online influences?

What difficulties and situations tempt you to put the actual work of parenting on hold? Write out your commitment to be the very best parent you can be *now*—even in the midst of exhaustion, financial struggles, and overcoming your own dysfunctional upbringing.

CONCLUSION

A New Day

Parenting is one of the most difficult things you will ever do, and yet it is also one of the most rewarding. Children are a blessing and a gift from God. When we invest in them and put them first, we end up becoming better people. We experience positive change in our own lives. We dump bad habits, bad influencers, and bad lifestyles, and we adopt a mentality of responsibility.

But while this life change is incredible, it's also incredibly difficult to come by. So many of us walk around with our own baggage from childhood. We point to absent parents, abandonment, abuse, and pivotal moments when we weren't taught how to be a man or woman, and we say: "I can't do this. I can't become a good father or mother when I never had good parents growing up."

It takes time to turn things around, and children—especially older children—may not respond to your new parenting ways immediately. But a seed planted is never wasted. Keep at it, day after day and year after year. You will make a difference. You will impact their lives.

Even if your child continues to make poor decisions, know that you are making a difference. You never know what might have happened in your child's life if you had never stepped up to the plate. You never know what impact you are making, even when it feels as if you're not getting through. Continue to plant the seeds of wisdom you have learned in this book.

As I reflect on my journey, I would not change many of the things I've experienced. The good and the bad shaped me into the father I have become. Over the years, I began to see my father's absence as God's protection. God knew the full story and had a different plan for my life. The anger toward my father is gone now because I know God was ultimately in control the whole time. Had I not experienced the pain of fatherlessness, I probably would not have developed my conviction to help fatherless children and adults. I might not have been as involved in my own children's lives had I not missed seeing my father at my games, birthdays, and graduations. I might not tell my children that I love them so often had I not gone through life without feeling my father's love. I have been able to give to my children and many other children what I did not receive from my father.

My father's absence shaped me into an unapologetic advocate for fatherhood and strong parenting. Our youth have become my life's mission. If going through my difficult journey with my father needed to happen to change the game for my descendants, then I would sign up again and again so they can see a different narrative in their family history. I dedicate this book to them so that when they read it, they know I had them in mind long before their existence. I pray they will continue the healthy, positive fathering foundation that I have strived to establish. You can be a great father. You can be a great mother. With the help of God, and with a bit of common sense and time, you will stop the cycle of destructive parenting in your family and help guide everyone to a new day.

Repairing a Destroyed Fence

I shared previously that I used to have some extremely disrespectful interactions with my high school sweetheart's father. As my heart changed, I began to understand the severity of my actions. Becoming a father also helped me to understand and respect his position. As time went on, I knew I needed to apologize to him and ask for his forgiveness.

In 2001, I picked up the phone and called him at his office. I didn't know how he would respond, considering it had been nearly ten years since we last spoke. When he answered the phone, I announced who I was. His response was cordial. I immediately told him that I was calling to apologize for my words and actions so many years ago. Then I asked for his forgiveness. To my surprise, he began to weep. I was stunned! Through his tears, he told me he forgave me and accepted my apology. I was speechless and in awe of what was happening. I knew something special was occurring.

It has been nearly twenty years since that conversation, yet it sticks with me to this day. It was a pivotal moment in my life as a man, husband, and father. I took complete responsibility for my actions, and grace was extended to me. I easily could have continued to live my life without making that phone call, but there was a blessing for both of us as a result of me picking up the phone.

The man who picked up the phone was the man I wanted to become. I no longer wanted to walk around harboring these offenses, and I was the only person who could release them. That day changed my life, and his as well, and I am forever grateful for the opportunity.

Andre

I met one of my sisters for the first time at my father's

funeral. When she saw me, she was stunned by my resemblance to our brother Andre. She and Andre share the same mother.

My sister informed me that Andre was incarcerated, but that didn't discourage me from wanting to meet him and establish a relationship. While my father could not be blamed for Andre's decisions, somehow my twenty-two-year-old mind knew that my father's absence in his life had contributed to his incarceration.

I sent Andre a letter, and shortly thereafter, he added me to his visitors list. He was only a two-hour drive away from my home in D.C., and I was excited to meet him, regardless of the fact that he was in prison. I didn't know what to expect, but I knew I was supposed to go see my brother. He was my brother, which was all that mattered.

When we met, it was obvious that we had chemistry. Although we didn't grow up together and he is six years older, we discovered that we shared a similar journey. Right away, we felt on many levels as if we were brothers who had actually grown up together. He was not due to be released for another five years, so we wrote letters and talked on the phone periodically, which gave us an opportunity to bond so that we weren't total strangers at the time of his release.

Y2K 1999

On New Year's Eve 1999, Andre surprised me by knocking on my door. I couldn't believe my brother was at my home! It was a surreal moment. He was the first sibling ever to visit my home.

As we talked, I quickly realized that although Andre was free, he would soon find himself in the same situation as before if he did not develop some skills to provide a sustainable, legal income. He was unemployed and working odd jobs to survive. In the past, his income came from detailing cars and selling drugs. He had dropped out of high school as a teen, beginning his street life from there. While in prison, however, he had earned his high school diploma.

As Andre shared stories about his children, I could not help but think about what would happen to them if he were taken away again. The cycle of fatherlessness would continue, and my father's deadbeat legacy would be passed down through another generation. I knew I needed to step in and do something. There was no way I was going to sit back and passively watch this happen again.

I was in the process of working on a house remodeling job in South Carolina. I wanted to see if Andre was really ready to change his life, or if he was just talking a good game but not ready to work. I offered him a job working with me on the house remodel in South Carolina for $500 a week. Andre accepted the offer and we headed to South Carolina. Little did either one of us know that this job would change both of our lives forever.

When I offered Andre the initial job, I wanted to see if he demonstrated hard work and commitment. Anyone who has worked with me closely knows that I work on a different level than most people. The bottom line is that I get the job done. If Andre could keep pace with me, I knew he was ready for the next step in the journey. Well, on one of those workdays, Andre outworked me. I was stunned.

Less than a week after the job ended, I offered Andre another job. I had the opportunity to invest $10,000 into starting a pressure washing company. This new opportunity would give him a chance to develop some additional skills. I offered him a free room in my basement, a weekly salary, and a complete pressure washing rig to execute the jobs. I was worried that he would end up incarcerated again if I didn't do something. What would happen to his children? What type of life would they have if they continued to grow up without him?

When I offered Andre this new opportunity, I expected him to jump at the chance. To my surprise, after taking three weeks to decide, he turned me down. He shared with me that it was largely the fear of the unknown. Additionally, we really didn't know each other, and it would be a big step for him to move from Portsmouth, Virginia, to Washington, D.C.. Portsmouth was familiar territory to him; I was asking him to trust me with uprooting and relocating his entire life. I respected him for pausing to think about it. Though it surprised me, his decision confirmed to me that I was right to be willing to make such a big investment in his life. He eventually decided to take a chance and move, and the rest is history.

In April of 2000, I started the pressure washing company with Andre as the lead man. Neither one of us knew anything about pressure washing, and there were no YouTube videos to watch for guidance. Several weeks before I officially launched the company, I reached out to a pressure washer dealer listed in the yellow pages for some advice. To my surprise, he offered to train Andre and me in the techniques and business of pressure washing for free.

Andre is really a one-of-a-kind person. I knew he would take this opportunity to the next level because of his overall positive attitude. He confronted his fears and challenges and conquered them. He paid his dues and turned his life completely around.

Today, Andre is the sole owner of his own pressure washing company. His two sons work for the company, and he has been involved in all four of his children's lives since he was released from prison in 1999. "Pa-Pa," as his grandchildren call him, has left a completely different legacy for them to follow now. The tarnished legacy we had been handed has been shattered.

Andre is married and owns multiple homes. He has a

work fleet of eight vehicles and has all of his certifications so that he can take advantage of the most lucrative pressure washing contracts. Every time I see one of his trucks or vans as I'm driving around, my heart smiles because I know the real story behind Sure Shot Pressure Washing.

Some might ask, how did I benefit? My goal was never exclusively to make money from the venture. My primary goal was to help my brother start a new life. This mission was accomplished, and I eventually moved on from pressure washing to pursue other interests. Ironically, because of my willingness to help Andre, he ended up introducing me to the most lucrative business venture of my life. Sometimes the willingness to help the right people pays dividends in ways we don't see coming.

Today, Andre and I both own very successful businesses and we still work with each other on various contracts. I can't help but wonder what both of our lives would look like if we had both made different decisions back in 2000. The beauty of this story is that we can pay it forward and know we are game changers for our family.

Leave a Legacy

In the summer of 2019, I decided to climb Mount Kilimanjaro. This decision was inspired by several factors, including that I wanted my children to see their father face and conquer a major, very tangible obstacle. Because I'm not a hiker and had never climbed a mountain before, this was particularly challenging. In order to reach the summit, I had to draw upon the memory of all of the mental challenges I had faced and overcome to remind me of what I could accomplish. The rejections I'd had to overcome, the fears and embarrassments I'd had to conquer, the feelings of defeat, the moments of depression, and the failures that had turned into victories—all propelled me to the top.

As I approached the Uhuru Peak at 19,341 feet, I

became very emotional—mindful that this was symbolic of my life on many levels. It was surreal and humbling to know that I had faced so much, yet had been afforded the opportunity to see a part of the world most people never experience. In that moment, I knew something positive had changed for my legacy.

I encourage you to use any challenges you may have faced as a springboard for your future parenting success. We can't change the past, but we can change the future for ourselves and for our children. Let this be the day you become that game changer and leave a legacy that your grandchildren will be proud of.

I also want to encourage you to find your own Mount Kilimanjaro and conquer it. It might not be a mountain. It can be anything that challenges you to a healthy breaking point. I'm not suggesting doing anything harmful. I am encouraging you to stretch yourself far beyond your comfort zone and enjoy the benefits of the experience.

As you move forward in your parenting journey, be encouraged! Even if your children are adults with their own children, you can still apply these strategies. Regardless of age, children always want the love and affirmation of their parents. Keep in mind, parenting is a life-long journey, and it is one of the most honorable responsibilities entrusted to us. Let's embrace it and give it our absolute best.

After all of the dysfunction that has been passed down through both sides of my family, I have made a conscious decision to be a game changer. While I have made mistakes as a father, and will continue to do so, I am fully aware of my role in setting a new standard. Although my earthly father didn't give me the tools I needed to be a good father, my heavenly Father has provided every tool I need.

Each day, I am learning something new, and it's encouraging. My children are a gift and need to be nurtured and loved.

Part of that love is discipline. Part of it is being present in their lives, even into adulthood. Part of it is saying no as often as I say yes.

Part of that love is instruction. Part of it is listening. Part of it is being corrected.

Part of that love is apologizing. Part of it is asking for forgiveness.

Part of that love is patience, and part of it is kindness. Part of it is a hug.

And part of that love is simply saying, "I love you."

Questions

1. How is modern culture influencing your parenting style?

2. Whom do you admire as a parent, and why?

3. Does your family need professional therapy? If so, when will you take action and set up an appointment?

4. Do you have a parent with whom you need to share your honest feelings? If so, what is your plan for sharing those feelings?

5. How is your present financial condition affecting your family in a positive and negative way?

6. Do you have adequate life insurance on yourself and your children? If not, why? Will you consider adding a policy that covers all of your family members?

7. Have you started saving for your children's future?

8. What are some dreams and goals you have for your family? Write them down!

Additional Resources

If you are looking for additional resources to support you in your parenting journey, you are encouraged to learn more from Jay with the following tools found at jaycameron.com:

1. The Maximum Impact Youth and Young Adult Success Online Academy (a Family Resource).

2. Empower Your Teen—the Secrets of Successful Parents.

3. The Debt Free College Degree Online Masterclass—How to Avoid Student Loans While Saving 60% to 70% off of the Cost of College.

4. The Financial Detox Online Masterclass—Remove the Junk and Establish a Solid Foundation for a Healthy Future.

5. Toxic Love—Ten Relationship Mistakes That Nearly Cost Me Everything.

About the Author

With a multi-faceted career that has spanned nearly thirty years, Jay Cameron possesses unique expertise as an entrepreneur, speaker, playwright, community leader, and philanthropist.

As a fatherless child, Jay's journey was not an easy one. Given a host of emotional, behavioral, and academic challenges, Jay's future was not promising. That is, until he was faced with a critical decision that changed the course of his life.

Today, Jay is a husband, father, and community leader who draws on his painful childhood, challenges, and mistakes to empower people around the globe.

Jay has founded three youth programs that focus on performing arts, life skills, and money management. He has also created personal development and parenting workshops, financial detox classes, and healthy relationships seminars and online courses.

Jay lives in suburban Washington, D.C., with his family. Jay has a strong belief in giving back so that others can avoid costly mistakes and live an accomplished life.

Made in the USA
Middletown, DE
16 July 2020